Onli

Congratulations! You now have access to practical templates of Python concepts that you will learn in this book. These downloadable templates will help you implement your learnings in the real world and give you an in-depth understanding of the concepts.

The templates feature a detailed **glossary of functions** that is divided into three sections: Python built-ins, built-in libraries, and third-party libraries. This glossary serves as a valuable reference, summarizing the technical functions discussed throughout the book. The glossary includes:

- A description of the function
- Syntax and parameters for every function
- Examples to illustrate the usage of each function

Additionally, you will have access to high-resolution images referenced throughout the book, as well as the code snippets discussed. You can directly use these code examples to see the results firsthand or adapt them to your own projects.

To access the templates, follow the steps below:

1. Go to www.vibrantpublishers.com
2. Click on the 'Online Resources' option on the Home Page
3. Login by entering your account details (or create an account if you don't have one)
4. Go to the Self-Learning Management series section on the Online Resources page
5. Click the 'Python Essentials You Always Wanted To Know' link and access the templates.

Happy self-learning!

This page is intentionally left blank

SELF-LEARNING MANAGEMENT SERIES

VIBRANT
PUBLISHERS

PYTHON ESSENTIALS

YOU ALWAYS WANTED TO KNOW

Learn python the easy way with no prior experience'

SHAWN PETERS

Python Essentials You Always Wanted To Know

First Edition

Paperback ISBN 10: 1-63651-293-3
Paperback ISBN 13: 978-1-63651-293-8

Ebook ISBN 10: 1-63651-294-1
Ebook ISBN 13: 978-1-63651-294-5

Hardback ISBN 10: 1-63651-295-X
Hardback ISBN 13: 978-1-63651-295-2

Library of Congress Control Number: 2024945458

This publication is designed to provide accurate and authoritative information in regard to the subject matter covered. The Author has made every effort in the preparation of this book to ensure the accuracy of the information. However, information in this book is sold without warranty either expressed or implied. The Author or the Publisher will not be liable for any damages caused or alleged to be caused either directly or indirectly by this book.

Vibrant Publishers books are available at special quantity discount for sales promotions, or for use in corporate training programs. For more information please write to bulkorders@vibrantpublishers.com

Please email feedback / corrections (technical, grammatical or spelling) to spellerrors@vibrantpublishers.com

To access the complete catalogue of Vibrant Publishers, visit www.vibrantpublishers.com

SELF-LEARNING MANAGEMENT SERIES

TITLE	PAPERBACK* ISBN
ACCOUNTING, FINANCE & ECONOMICS	
COST ACCOUNTING AND MANAGEMENT ESSENTIALS	9781636511030
FINANCIAL ACCOUNTING ESSENTIALS	9781636510972
FINANCIAL MANAGEMENT ESSENTIALS	9781636511009
MACROECONOMICS ESSENTIALS	9781636511818
MICROECONOMICS ESSENTIALS	9781636511153
PERSONAL FINANCE ESSENTIALS	9781636511849
PRINCIPLES OF ECONOMICS ESSENTIALS	9781636512334
COMPUTER SCIENCE	
BLOCKCHAIN ESSENTIALS	9781636513003
DATA ANALYTICS ESSENTIALS	9781636511184
PYTHON ESSENTIALS	9781636512938
ENTREPRENEURSHIP & STRATEGY	
BUSINESS COMMUNICATION ESSENTIALS	9781636511634
BUSINESS PLAN ESSENTIALS	9781636511214
BUSINESS STRATEGY ESSENTIALS	9781949395778
ENTREPRENEURSHIP ESSENTIALS	9781636511603
GENERAL MANAGEMENT	
BUSINESS LAW ESSENTIALS	9781636511702
DECISION MAKING ESSENTIALS	9781636510026
INDIA'S ROAD TO TRANSFORMATION: WHY LEADERSHIP MATTERS	9781636512273
LEADERSHIP ESSENTIALS	9781636510316
PRINCIPLES OF MANAGEMENT ESSENTIALS	9781636511542
TIME MANAGEMENT ESSENTIALS	9781636511665

*Also available in Hardback & Ebook formats

SELF-LEARNING MANAGEMENT SERIES

TITLE	PAPERBACK* ISBN

HUMAN RESOURCE MANAGEMENT

TITLE	PAPERBACK ISBN
DIVERSITY, EQUITY, AND INCLUSION ESSENTIALS	9781636512976
DIVERSITY IN THE WORKPLACE ESSENTIALS	9781636511122
HR ANALYTICS ESSENTIALS	9781636510347
HUMAN RESOURCE MANAGEMENT ESSENTIALS	9781949395839
ORGANIZATIONAL BEHAVIOR ESSENTIALS	9781636510378
ORGANIZATIONAL DEVELOPMENT ESSENTIALS	9781636511481

MARKETING & SALES MANAGEMENT

TITLE	PAPERBACK ISBN
DIGITAL MARKETING ESSENTIALS	9781949395747
MARKETING MANAGEMENT ESSENTIALS	9781636511783
SALES MANAGEMENT ESSENTIALS	9781636510743
SERVICES MARKETING ESSENTIALS	9781636511733
SOCIAL MEDIA MARKETING ESSENTIALS	9781636512181

OPERATIONS & PROJECT MANAGEMENT

TITLE	PAPERBACK ISBN
AGILE ESSENTIALS	9781636510057
OPERATIONS & SUPPLY CHAIN MANAGEMENT ESSENTIALS	9781949395242
PROJECT MANAGEMENT ESSENTIALS	9781636510712
STAKEHOLDER ENGAGEMENT ESSENTIALS	9781636511511

*Also available in Hardback & Ebook formats

About the Author

Shawn Peters is an experienced educator with a passion for technology. He has a Bachelor of Science degree with a major in Physics and a minor in Mathematics from Memorial University of Newfoundland and spent the beginning of his teaching career focusing on science and mathematics education. Recently he has begun focusing more on his love of programming gradually shifting his focus from science and mathematics to teaching computer science, and received certification from the College of the North Atlantic in Python Programming Teaching.

In addition to his 19 years as a junior and senior high school educator, Shawn also works in curriculum development and as a freelance programmer specializing in Python, JavaScript, and Java. His recent journey into programming was fueled by his lifelong passion for the subject. As a child, he started programming in GW-Basic and QBasic, and working with HTML for simple website design, but never pursued a formal education. Throughout his teaching career, Shawn found ways to incorporate programming into his teaching methods and began exploring programming in a more comprehensive way, gradually shifting from teaching science and mathematics and focusing more on technology courses.

Shawn enjoys creating artwork with JavaScript and p5.js that incorporate mathematical and physics concepts into their creation. He also specializes in developing applications in Python, with a focus on puzzle-generating software.

What experts say about this book!

Python Essentials You Always Wanted to Know by Shawn Peters provides a brilliant approach to learning Python. It not only moves you through all aspects of programming in Python, but also focuses on using the language to address and solve problems efficiently.

Its approach is novel as it encourages the reader to play a lead role in breaking down and thinking through problems and provides expert guidance on how to do this. It also includes quizzes with answers so that you can test yourself on what you've learned.

You can read the book from front to back or jump to whatever aspect of programming based on your needs. Whether you're a novice programmer or an experienced programmer looking to advance your coding skills or approach to problem-solving in Python, you're going to appreciate this book.

– Sandra Henry
Stocker, NetworkWorld

This book offers a beginner-friendly approach to learning Python, focusing not only on syntax but also on problem-solving, which is key for effective programming. The author's clear intent is to make coding enjoyable and relevant, providing examples that are simple yet significant to help readers follow along. The emphasis is on applying coding skills practically, with quizzes and case studies included to solidify your understanding. By the end, readers will have a solid grasp of essential concepts such as Python syntax, data structures, error handling, and object-oriented programming, all while gaining the confidence to solve real-world problems. After having an understanding of these concepts, you will be well-prepared to tackle more advanced Python topics and apply your skills to real-life coding challenges.

– LooYee NG
Solutions Architect at CTMG

What experts say about this book!

What a great introduction to this topic, especially for a non-programmer like myself! The examples provided are easy to understand and apply, allowing me to try it out for myself to further cement my understanding of the steps involved. Read, See, Do. A great way to learn. I really enjoyed the quizzes at the end of each chapter, as they emphasized what the important takeaways were and reinforced what I did know - and what I didn't. I'll probably never become a programmer, but understanding how programming works is an asset to any user.

– Sharon Peach
B.Sc, B.Ed, M.Ed

This page is intentionally left blank

Table of Contents

10 Next Steps and Further Resources 253

Glossary 267

Bibliography 277

Preface

I grew up in a time when the internet was yet to be. I enjoyed technology in all of its forms and I always tried to keep up with the latest trends and ideas, and then the internet happened. I was amazed and excited at the rapid development of technology, but I was also afraid. Not in a "technology will take over the world" kind of way, but in a "how can I ever hope to keep up" kind of way. I had hoped to work in technology and had my heart set on designing video games, but the rapid paradigm shift in the world left me shaken. I dropped my dreams of programming, afraid that I would become obsolete before I could even finish school, and fell back on my secondary choice, teaching science and mathematics.

So why am I now writing a book on programming? The short answer is that my love of programming never departed, despite never completing a degree in computer science. In teaching, I kept trying to find resources that would help in my classes and decided that it would be easier to just do it myself. I taught myself to program, started making some simple resources, and eventually started teaching technology courses.

The longer answer is that I'm afraid again. I'm afraid that AI software is going to scare people the way that the internet scared me. Again, not that the technology itself is frightening, but that the rapid development that it represents may keep people away from pursuing a career in technology. If you've ever had an interest in programming, but fear kept you aware, this is a book for you. Maybe you thought you needed a strong math background. Maybe you thought there were no jobs for programmers. Maybe you thought it was too late for you to start. Regardless of why you haven't learned to program, we can start here now together.

Introduction to the Book

This is not a traditional computer science book. This is about learning the why as much as it is about the how. I want you to learn how to approach problems that you would like to solve and how to apply programming to efficiently solve them. Here you will learn to think like a programmer while learning the skills necessary to code in Python.

This book starts with the assumption that you have never written a line of code in your life. In this book, you will learn the basics of Python, and even touch on some more advanced topics that you may want to explore further after reading this book. Python itself is a generalized language, and can really be used to write code that does pretty much anything, so it would be impossible to include everything that Python is capable of in one book. In choosing the topics, I really thought about what you, as a beginner, would need to know to be able to write your own programs. I also wanted to give you a taste of what you might see if you continue learning to code. I truly believe that this book will give you a solid foundation to begin your programming journey.

I personally despise boring code. While syntax is important and it is certainly important to learn about efficient algorithms, the focus here will be on problem-solving. In the beginning chapters, you will find lots of examples to illustrate the key concepts that you can follow along with. Wherever possible, the examples are kept simple while still being relevant. In each section, you will find quizzes and answers to test your general knowledge, but the real test is understanding and working with the code.

As you progress through the book, the topics will increase in difficulty, but you will still find the relevant examples to guide you on your way. There are also several case studies included near the end of the book which I highly recommend attempting to solve on your own first.

By the end of this book, you should understand:

- Basic Python syntax

- Working with different data types and data structures

- Writing your own functions and importing functions from other libraries

- How to handle errors in programs

- What object-oriented programming is, and how to use it

- How to analyze data

- How to solve real-world problems using Python

- How to move forward on your programming journey

Who can benefit from this book?

1. Beginners with little to no programming experience.

2. Students, at the high school or undergraduate level, who want to learn practical programming skills.

3. Professionals from non-technical backgrounds who want to gain an understanding of Python programming.

4. Professionals who want to transition into roles requiring basic programming skills, such as data analysis, web development, or automation.

5. Hobbyists and enthusiasts, eager to explore coding through Python.

6. Educators and instructors looking for a comprehensive resource to teach Python programming in a clear and accessible manner.

How to use this book?

This book is designed to be flexible and adaptable to your learning style and goals, however here are some suggestions on how to make the most of this book.

Start from the beginning: If you are new to programming, we recommend starting with Chapter 1 and reading the book sequentially. This will help provide a solid foundation in Python fundamentals. If you have experience with programming, you could skip the first chapter, however, there are some great examples of setting up flowcharts and pseudocode that you won't want to miss.

Focus on specific topics: Already know the basics? Maybe jump to Chapter 4 to learn more about functions or Chapter 5 to learn about object-oriented programming. Running into errors? Maybe check Chapter 7 on error handling. Keep in mind however that the chapters do build on each other, so you may need to reference back.

Work backward from the case studies: Maybe you like to learn by applying skills. The case studies in Chapter 8 apply information from the book in order. Case study 1 deals with content from Chapters 2 – 4. Case study 2 is mostly focused on chapter 5 and case study 3 deals with content from chapter 7.

Regardless of how you choose to progress through this book, it would be a good idea to follow along with the activities. If you have a PDF copy of the book, you can copy and paste it into a code editor, however, it is better practice to type the code out yourself for the experience. Making small changes to the code examples to see the impacts on the output is also a great way to gain experience.

This page is intentionally left blank

Chapter 1

Thinking Like a Programmer

This chapter covers the fundamental aspects of programming, not just for programmers but for all people. We will investigate the underlying principles of programming, as well as its importance in our modern lives. We will explore Python as a beginner-friendly language to start our programming journey. Before learning to program in Python, we will investigate how to think like a programmer and how to use tools like pseudocode and flowcharts to make it easier to understand and communicate about programming.

The key learning objectives of this chapter are:

- Understanding the significance of programming skills in today's digital age

- Recognizing Python as a versatile and beginner-friendly programming language

- Understanding programmatic thinking and apply it to everyday situations

- Utilizing pseudocode and flowcharts to plan and visualize algorithms

1.1 The Importance of Learning Programming

Technology plays a major role in all areas of our lives. It is ubiquitous in that it has become so much of a part of our lives that we no longer really notice it. Most people do not really consider what kind of effort goes into creating and maintaining the technology that is all around us. Even though we live in a technology-centered world, many people do not even consider a career in technology. In my own case, I initially avoided pursuing a technology-based education as there was too much mystery and uncertainty involved. After all, I was born into a pre-internet world and was set to graduate high school in the midst of an Internet revolution. Overwhelmed doesn't begin to describe it. I imagine that regardless of when you were born, the technology of the day has a mystery to it, and peeking behind the veil is a scary concept. How could we possibly work with these new technologies while they are still changing and evolving? How could we possibly hope to stay relevant when there will always be younger and more integrated candidates coming up through the education system?

If you are curious about *programming* and related computer topics but are unsure where to start, learning the basics is your best first step. I would argue that regardless of your interest level, gaining a beginner's level of comfort with programming is essential. Much like literacy and numeracy, the ability to understand and manipulate code has become a valuable skill set. We stand at the edge of yet another technological revolution with the integration of artificial intelligence into daily life, and without understanding the underlying technology, we risk trusting it infallibly. Working with computer systems through programming can give us an appreciation of how such systems can be created, and also how they can be biased and flawed.

Learning programming offers a multitude of benefits, both personally and professionally, making it an essential pursuit in the 21st century. From the apps on our smartphones to the algorithms powering social media feeds, programming underpins much of the technology we interact with daily. By learning to code, we can gain insights into how these technologies function, empowering us to navigate the digital landscape more effectively and make informed decisions about the tools we use.

At its core, programming is about problem-solving. Whether it's automating routine tasks, analyzing complex datasets, or building innovative software solutions, programming equips individuals with the tools and techniques to tackle a wide range of challenges. By honing our problem-solving skills through programming, we can become more adept at breaking down complex problems, devising efficient solutions, and implementing them effectively—a valuable asset in any profession.

Proficiency in programming not only unlocks a wealth of career opportunities spanning various industries but also serves as a gateway to economic empowerment in today's digital landscape. The demand for programming skills extends far beyond traditional software development roles, encompassing areas such as data analysis, cybersecurity, and artificial intelligence. With these skills, individuals can position themselves for lucrative and fulfilling careers, characterized by ample opportunities for professional growth and advancement.

Moreover, programming proficiency offers a pathway to economic empowerment amid the evolving digital economy. As industries increasingly rely on technology-driven solutions, the demand for skilled professionals capable of developing and maintaining these systems is skyrocketing. By acquiring programming skills, individuals can access higher-paying job prospects, attain financial stability, and actively contribute to economic prosperity.

While it should be noted that traditional computer programming roles may be on the decline in the United States, related fields such as Computer and Information Research Scientists and Software Developers, Quality Assurance Analysts, and Testers are experiencing accelerated growth rates, surpassing the average job market expansion. Companies need workers who can understand, write, and more importantly apply code.

Programming is about more than just writing line after line of code. While programming is often, at its core, about solving problems, it is important to understand that there is not just one solution to most problems. Just like real-world issues, solving problems in programming is more about finding a solution that works for you. If you were to give several programmers a task, they may all come back with different solutions to the problem. Some may take less time while others may be more efficient in terms of memory, but many of them will be valid solutions.

Programming is ultimately about bringing your ideas into reality using code as a medium. This could be creating a mobile app as part of a software development team, or a portfolio website to highlight your programming skills. It could be looking at unique ways to tackle real-world challenges, or it could be engaging in creative coding.

Knowledge changes so quickly in today's world that what we learn can be out of date faster than we can use it. Learning new skills and adapting to change is a much more important endeavor. Learning programming can help with skill development through continuous learning. There is always something new to learn, and more importantly to apply in the quickly evolving world of programming. This culture of growth and development extends beyond just programming. Soft skills are those skills that we learn that extend beyond pure content. Communication, teamwork, and problem-solving are essential to programmers but are essential in many other fields as well. Learning to communicate with colleagues, especially those who might not understand the technical jargon, can be applied to many other fields of work. Likewise, teamwork skills gained by collaborating on larger projects and problem-solving skills gained by analyzing and solving difficult programming problems are extremely important in other areas as well.

Generative art and *creative coding* further underscore the role of programming in nurturing creativity and innovation. Generative art involves using algorithms to create art autonomously. The artist creates rules and guidelines for the system and then allows the system to create visually stunning and thought-provoking artworks. For example, Figure 1.1 uses a flocking algorithm to move and trace the path of particles, whereas Figure 1.2 uses a genetic algorithm to progressively evolve toward a goal, in this case creating a representation of the letter L. This should not be confused with AI art generated with a single prompt but is a complex intertwining of art and code

Figure 1.1 Certain Neighborhoods

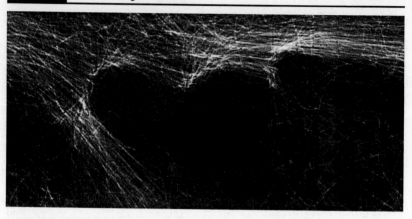

Figure 1.2 Evolving Typography

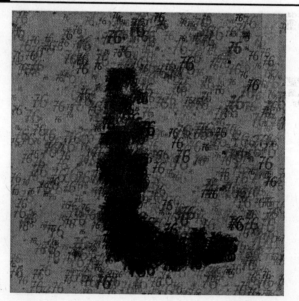

Creative coding is a fusion of programming and artistic expression that enables individuals to develop complex artworks, interactive exhibits, and multimedia experiences. By mixing art, mathematics, science, and computer science, coding is a powerful tool for unleashing creative potential and inspiring transformative artworks.

1.2 Python — A Beginner Friendly Language

As we begin our programming journey, we have important questions to answer. Which programming language should we learn? Which is the best programming language? Which will give us the best employment opportunities?

One way to approach these problems is to look at the popularity of programming languages. While specific needs may vary across various disciplines and sectors, analysis of engineering job postings has revealed that MATLAB, Python, and C++ are among the most sought-after programming languages by employers.[1] Employability is fine, but if the languages are too complex for beginners that will not help us start our journey.

Figure 1.3 shows the popularity of programming languages based on search engine queries. Again, we can see Python ranking at the top.

---

1. Lisa Schibelius, Amanda Ross, and Andrew Katz, "An Empirical Study of Programming Languages Specified in Engineering Job Postings" (American Society for Engineering Education, 2022)

| **Figure 1.3** | **Popularity of Programming Languages based on the TIOBE index[2]** |

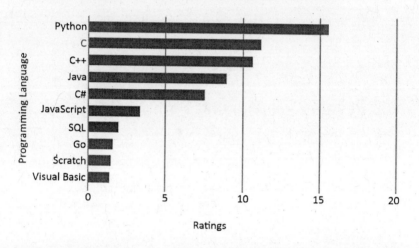

Python has emerged as a popular programming language due to its simplicity, versatility, and readability. Widely used across various domains, including web development, data analysis, artificial intelligence, automation, and more, Python offers several benefits:

- **Simplicity:** Python's clear and concise syntax makes it an ideal choice for beginners, enabling them to write code that is easy to read and understand.

- **Versatility:** Python supports a wide range of programming styles and project types, making it suitable for solving diverse problems.

- **Abundance of Libraries:** Python boasts a vast ecosystem of libraries and frameworks that extend its capabilities,

2. TIOBE Software BV. "TIOBE Index for March 2024." Accessed March 12, 2024. https://www.tiobe.com/tiobe-index/

allowing programmers to leverage existing tools and resources for their projects.

- **Community Support:** With a large and active community of developers, educators, and enthusiasts, Python offers a supportive environment for learning and collaboration.

By learning Python, individuals gain access to a powerful toolset for problem-solving, creativity, and innovation. Whether you're a complete beginner or a seasoned programmer looking to expand your skill set, Python provides a welcoming entry point into the world of programming. Moreover, the skills acquired in Python can be applied to other programming languages, facilitating the transition between different technologies and domains.

Python is an interpreted language, which means that we need software to translate our code into machine code so that the computer can understand and execute it. Our code needs to be interpreted each time it is run, so each computer that will run the code will need a Python interpreter installed. To avoid issues with setup, I will be recommending the use of an online IDE, or integrated development environment, which will include the interpreter as well as a code editor. The code editor is typically just a text editor with some extra features built in to make it easier to work with. There are many available online for free, but I will be recommending using replit (https://replit.com/) as it will support everything that is needed to follow along with this book without supplying too many additional features that can be distracting for beginners.

If you are more interested in working with Python offline, you will need to download the interpreter from the Python website (https://www.python.org/) and, unless you want to use a text editor, an IDE. While Visual Studio Code is a popular multiple-language IDE that is certainly worth checking out, it can be intimidating for beginners. Beginners might want to start with a Python specific IDE like IDLE, Thonny, or PyCharm. More information on setting up Python on your own computer can be found in the appendix.

1.3 Programming and Programmatic Thinking

Before we start writing code, it's crucial to understand the spirit of programming. As previously discussed, programming is more than just writing code. Programming includes designing, testing, and maintaining code to develop software applications, *scripts*, or *algorithms*. Similar to a sculptor crafting a masterpiece, having a well though-out, highly structured plan is key in programming. Without such a plan, the work may end up flawed, requiring time to go back and fix mistakes, or in the worst case scenario, a complete restart. Therefore, understanding the problem at hand and devising a plan of action are essential components of the process. This structured approach is called *programmatic thinking*. It involves analyzing problems, identifying patterns, and devising step-by-step instructions to solve them. Programmatic thinking demands a logical mindset. We need to learn to think in terms of sequences, *conditions*, *loops*, and *functions* to take on various challenges. However, creativity also holds significance in programming, as it complements logical thinking by allowing programmers to explore new solutions and approach problems from different angles.

Understanding programmatic thinking is critical as it enables individuals to address problems systematically. We need to break large problems down into logical steps that can be implemented using programming languages like Python. By applying programmatic thinking, we can develop efficient solutions to problems that seem simple, like automating replies to emails, to the most complex problems such as managing appointment bookings to minimize wait times for hospitals.

To understand programmatic thinking, let's investigate the development of a mobile banking application. The development team must determine what features need to be included and how users will interact with the software. Furthermore, they must consider the security measures to keep user data safe and protect user accounts. They also must make sure that the new app integrates with the current banking systems. This is before writing a single line of code. If they just started coding without a plan, they could introduce a security risk that could require them to restart the project from scratch.

Regardless of what we code, programming will give us a new toolkit to take on problems. Programming skills can allow us to take on problems head-on and start creating solutions that affect our daily lives. You don't need to become a programmer to use programming. As professionals, we can find ways to streamline our workflows by leveraging programming. Think of the repetitive tasks that could be automated to save time in your workplace. Whether it is in finance, healthcare, or education, professionals equipped with problem-solving and programming skills, can address the challenges that limit efficiency in the workplace.

1.4 Pseudocode and Flowcharts

Pseudocode and *flowcharts* are invaluable tools in the world of programming, serving as bridges between human understanding and computer logic. They provide a structured way to plan and visualize the steps needed to solve a problem before diving into actual coding.

Pseudocode, as the name suggests, is a "pseudo" or imitation of code. It uses natural language mixed with some basic programming ideas to outline the logic of the solution. Pseudocode allows programmers to focus on the logic of their algorithms without getting bogged down in language-specific details and serves as a blueprint for writing actual code later on.

This offers two major benefits. First, since it is not language-specific, pseudocode can be written once and applied to many different programming languages later. Second, since pseudocode resembles human language it is easier for people without programming experience to understand. Since programming large projects involves many different parties, this can improve the ability for communication between all team members, regardless of their coding background.

As an example, many people have trouble figuring out someone's precise age, depending on if their birthday month has passed yet. In written word, this is how the problem can be approached.

First of all, we would make sure we know the current date and their date of birth. A little subtraction gives us an approximate age. Next, we have to determine if they have already had their birthday this year. If they have, then the number we have is correct. If not, we need to subtract one from our answer to get their exact age.

From this simple example, we can see several key concepts in programming. Note the sequential nature of the steps. In programming, steps must be written in a logical order. We have to obtain the necessary information, and cannot assume that we simply have it. When writing programs, making assumptions can introduce a lot of errors into our programs. We can also see some branching in these instructions: sometimes we subtract 1, sometimes we do not.

While programming does not need to be highly mathematical, it is important to understand some basic concepts. To simplify the pseudocode, the symbols for greater than (>) and less than (<) are typically used. This is also heavily used in most, if not all, programming languages.

Here are the same instructions written in pseudocode:

```
START

GET current year, current month, and current date
GET birth year, birth month, and birth date
SET age to current year subtract birth year

IF current month < birth month
    SET age to age subtract 1
ENDIF

ELSEIF current month = birth month and current date <
birth date
    SET age to age subtract 1
ENDELSEIF

DISPLAY age

END
```

Everyone has their own preferences when writing pseudocode and there is no single correct way to do so, but there are some common practices. Keywords are often written in all caps, but strictly speaking do not need to be. Indentation and spaces are used to separate sections. While it would seem strange to be this specific when giving a set of instructions to a person, computers interpret instructions exactly as written, line by line.

The ENDIF and ENDELSEIF statements are somewhat optional since the indentation lets us know what is included, but they are typically included to explicitly show that we are done with the section.

Common phrases that you may see include:

READ, OBTAIN, or GET for inputs.
PRINT, DISPLAY, or SHOW for outputs.
COMPUTE, CALCULATE, or DETERMINE for calculations.
SET or INIT for setting values.
INCREMENT or BUMP for increasing a value by one, a common process.[3]

It is worth noting that while pseudocode resembles code in structure, it cannot be understood by a computer. It is primarily an organizational tool for people.

While pseudocode offers a written interpretation of code, flowcharts offer a graphical representation of an algorithm or process. They use standardized symbols and arrows to depict the flow of control through a series of interconnected steps. Flowcharts are particularly useful for visual learners or when communicating algorithms to a broader audience. Flowcharts

---

3. Dr. John Dalbey. "Pseudocode Standard." Accessed March 20, 2024. https://users.csc. calpoly.edu/~jdalbey/SWE/pdl_std.html

make it easier to understand code and debug issues before coding starts by providing a clear, visual representation of the logic and flow of a program.

Figure 1.4 **Pseudocode symbols**

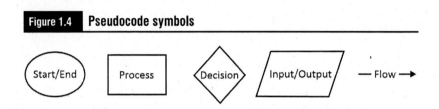

We use ellipses to indicate where we start and end the program. Rectangles are used to indicate processes completed by the computer. This can include setting values, doing calculations, or any other action the computer takes without direct user interaction. Decisions are represented in rhombi. We have seen some of these already such as if and else if in our pseudocode. Input is typically user interaction in the form of entered values, mouse interaction, or microphone information. Output can be in the form of text, images, or audio, among other things. These are represented in parallelograms. The flow of logic is represented by arrows.

Similar to pseudocode, exactly how a flowchart is laid out depends on the person making it, but there should be a sensible flow to it. Arrows should not cross and elements should be distributed in such a way that the path is clear.

Returning to our age example:

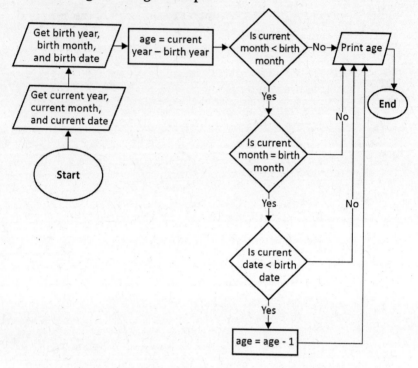

This clearly shows the sequential nature of the code to be written as well as the branching that occurs when determining if the person's birthday has currently passed.

Together, pseudocode and flowcharts form a powerful duo for problem-solving and algorithm design. They enable programmers to plan their solutions methodically, breaking down complex problems into manageable steps. By outlining the logic and flow of a program beforehand, developers can identify potential issues and design more efficient algorithms. In addition, these methods of organization can also allow for easier communication between all members of a team. Programming, especially in software development, is not typically a solo endeavor and not all team members will understand programming. By having an easier method to communicate ideas, everyone can more easily be on the same page.

Leaving our age example behind, let's focus on a more computer specific example. We will explore how to determine if a number is even or odd. This is a trivial example, but will help solidify the ideas.

From grade school mathematics, we should know that once we have a number, we need to see if it is divisible by two. We know a number is even if dividing it by two yields a remainder of zero.

In pseudocode:

```
START

OBTAIN number

IF number divided by 2 is 0
   OUTPUT "even"
ENDIF

ELSE
   OUTPUT "odd"
ENDELSE

END
```

In flowchart:

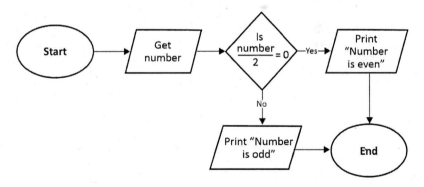

This might seem too simple, since we learn the difference between even and odd numbers at an early age, but we can apply this logic to any number of situations. While the pseudocode is simple for anyone to understand, here is the pseudocode represented in various programming languages.

Even and odd with Python code

Commands

```python
number = int(input("Enter a number: "))
if number % 2 ==0:
    print("even")
else:
    print("odd")
```

Output

```
Enter a number: 4
even
```

Even and odd with JavaScript code

Commands

```javascript
let number = parseInt(prompt("Enter a number: "));
if (number % 2 === 0) {
    console.log("even");
} else {
    console.log("odd")
}
```

Output

```
Enter a number: 7
odd
```

Even and odd with Java code

Commands

```java
import java.util.Scanner;
public class EvenOddChecker {
    public static void main(String[] args) {
        Scanner scanner = new Scanner(System.in);
        System.out.print("Enter a number: ");
        int number = scanner.nextInt();
        if (number % 2 == 0) {
            System.out.println("even");
        } else {
            System.out.println("odd");
        }
        scanner.close();
    }
}
```

Output

```
Enter a number: 28
even
```

Even and odd with C++ code

Commands

```
#include <iostream>
using namespace std;

int main() {
    int number;
    cout << "Enter a number: ";
    cin >> number;
    if (number % 2 == 0) {
        cout << "even" << endl;
    } else {
        cout << "odd" << endl;
    }
    return 0;
}
```

Output

```
Enter a number: 15
odd
```

While each version of the code looks different, it should be evident that they all represent the pseudocode and flowchart.

In the next chapter, we will be beginning our journey into Python programming, but we will continue revisiting pseudocode and flowcharts, exploring their use cases and best practices for effective problem-solving and algorithm design.

Quiz

1. **Which term describes the structured approach of analyzing problems, identifying patterns, and devising step-by-step instructions to solve them?**

    a. Pseudocode

    b. Programmatic thinking

    c. Flowchart

    d. Algorithm

2. **What is a significant advantage of using Python programming language?**

    a. Platform-specific limitations

    b. Slower execution speed compared to other languages

    c. High learning curve for beginners

    d. Wide range of libraries and frameworks for various tasks

3. **Which is NOT a benefit of using pseudocode**

    a. It is language-specific

    b. It helps in communication between team members

    c. It resembles human language

    d. It allows focusing on logic rather than syntax

4. **What does a rectangle represent in a flowchart?**

    a. Input

    b. Output

    c. Decision

    d. Process completed by the computer

5. **Which symbol is used to represent decisions in a flowchart?**
   a. Ellipses
   b. Rectangles
   c. Rhombi
   d. Parallelograms

6. **Where would you expect to find an ellipse in a flowchart?**
   a. At the beginning or end
   b. At decision points
   c. At inputs
   d. At outputs

7. **In the flowchart, what does "Get number" represent?**

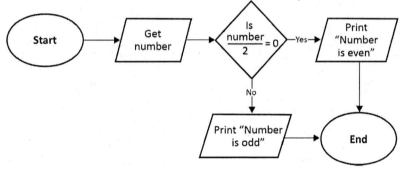

   a. Decision
   b. Flow
   c. Process
   d. Input/output

8. **In designing a flowchart to represent a complex decision-making process, which of the following considerations is most crucial?**

   a. Ensuring clarity and readability of the flowchart

   b. Ensuring scalability and adaptability

   c. Incorporating advanced programming concepts

   d. Minimizing the number of decision points

9. **Which phrase is commonly used in pseudocode to increase a value by one?**

   a. READ

   b. PRINT

   c. INCREMENT

   d. COMPUTE

10. **The pseudocode keyword GET would match up with which shape in a flowchart?**

    a. Ellipses

    b. Rectangles

    c. Rhombi

    d. Parallelograms

Answers	1 – b	2 – d	3 – a	4 – d	5 – c
	6 – a	7 – d	8 – a	9 – c	10 – d

Chapter Summary

◆ Programming influences everything in today's world from smartphone apps to online algorithms.

◆ Programming is more than just writing code and involves problem-solving skills, creativity, and innovation.

◆ Programming is essential for success across various domains, not just software-related fields.

◆ Python is a versatile and beginner-friendly programming language and is ideal for learners of all backgrounds and interests.

◆ Pseudocode and flowcharts are indispensable tools for planning and visualizing solutions and can improve communication and collaboration

This page is intentionally left blank

Chapter 2

Getting Started with Python

This chapter covers the basic syntax of programming in Python. We will explore the fundamentals of Python by outputting information to the screen and getting keyboard input. We will add variety and complexity to our code by learning about variables, conditional statements and loops. There's a lot to take in during this chapter but it will serve as an excellent foundation for us to continue building our programming skills

The key learning objectives of this chapter are:

- Understanding the general syntax of Python

- Utilizing functions such as `print()`, `input()`, and `type()`

- Understanding and utilizing data types and variables

- Using conditional logic to branch code

- Understanding and utilizing the different types of loops in Python

2.1 Syntax and Fundamentals

Hello World! ¡Hola Mundo! 你好，世界! All languages have their own unique ways of expressing ideas and have rules for what is understood. We may invite someone to observe the setting sun by saying "Look, a bright orange sunset" but you would never say "Look, a setting of sun orange bright" or as the French say "Regarde, un coucher de soleil orange vif." Like human language, programming languages have their own way of understanding what is written. What is understood by one language will not necessarily work for another.

Understanding how we communicate with computers can be a confusing topic. Machine language is a series of 0s and 1s that represent instructions and data that control a computer's hardware. While it is possible to write in machine language, it is highly impractical and next to impossible to proof read. In order to overcome this divide between human language and machine language, we use programming languages.

In the case of Python, we translate our human language into the *syntax* of Python. This still resembles English and is very readable and expressive, but can be more easily translated into machine language. Python is like an interpreter allowing us to communicate our ideas to the computer.

When we run a program written in Python, the Python interpreter translates the Python code into bytecode, which is an intermediate step to produce instructions that can be understood on any device. This bytecode is then translated into machine language based on the type of computer the code is being run on

Figure 2.1   Using Python to communicate with computers

Just like it would be difficult to explain what it means to write or speak English, it is tricky to simply write Python, or any programming language, into a few basic ideas; however, here are some important ideas.

- **Statements:** Python programs are composed of *statements*. Each statement performs a specific task or operation. There are many things we can do in statements that we will investigate later.

- **Indentation and whitespace:** In Python the spacing of characters are important. *Indentation* is used to show which pieces of code are blocked together. Statements are ended by pressing enter on the keyboard, known as a hard return.

- **Functions and methods:** Python has many built in *functions* and methods that can be used in statements. We will start by looking at the `print()` function. Functions can be used to simplify the flow of our code and make it more readable.

Python functions have names that are written without spaces. According to the PEP 8 (Python Enhancement Propossal version 8), function names should be lowercase. If more than one word is required, underscores should be used to separate them, as spaces are not allowed. Some function names may also be written in *mixed case* (often stylized as mixedCase), using capital letters to indicate the next word.[4] This will be more important when we

---

4. PEP 8, "PEP 8 -Style Guide for Python Code," Python.org, accessed April 20, 2024, https://peps.python.org/pep-0008/.

write our own functions, but for now we should expect to see both used when we read other programmer's code.

Functions in Python are followed by a set of parentheses. Inside of the parentheses, we include *arguments* that are passed into the function. Some arguments are required, while others are optional. Some functions do not even need arguments, but the parentheses must be included. The functions use arguments to define *parameters*, which act as placeholders for values that will be provided when the function is called. Within the function body, these parameters are then used to perform computations, manipulate data, or execute specific tasks based on the provided arguments. Parameters allow functions to be more flexible and reusable, as they can operate on different sets of data without needing to be rewritten for each use case. Some functions return information back to the program.

In Python, `print()` is a built-in function used to display output to the console. The official Python documentation specifies that the syntax for print is `print(*objects, sep=' ', end='\n', file=None, flush=False)`.[5] While this may seem complicated, print takes in any number of objects to print (*objects) and has several optional arguments. The optional arguments have equal signs with a default value supplied, and we will look into `sep`, short for separation, and `end`. The print function does not return any information.

Print is a versatile function and can handle many types of data, but we are going to start out with *strings*. Strings can be understood as characters, words, and sentences surrounded by quotation marks. Python accepts both single and double quotes, but they must be used in pairs.

---

5. Python Documentation, "Built-in Functions – Python 3.12.3 documentation accessed April 21, 2024, https://docs.python.org/3/library/functions.html

Example of print statements

Statement

```
print("Hello World")
print("Hello", "World")
print("First phrase", "Second phrase", "Third phrase")
```

Output

```
Hello World
Hello World
First phrase Second phrase Third phrase
```

By default, the arguments are separated by a single space, but this can be changed by using the optional argument sep. Optional arguments are included at the end of required arguments and are typically explicitly named with an equal sign

Example of print statements using various separations

Statement

```
print("Hello", "World", sep = "-")
print("Monday", "Tuesday", "Wednesday", sep="|")
print("1","2","3",sep = '..')
```

Output

```
Hello-World
Monday|Tuesday|Wednesday
1..2..3
```

We can also use the optional end argument to change what happens after the print function puts output to the screen. Referring to the documentation, we can see that by default it is \n. When we use a backslash like this, it is referred to as an escape character. Escape characters tell Python that the next character has a different meaning than is normally expected. In this case \n tells Python not to type the letter "n", but to start a new line. We often call this a hard return.

Fun Fact

There are many special characters including \t for a tab, \r to go back to the beginning of the line, \' or \" for literal quotation marks, or \\ for a literal backslash.

Example of print statements using various endings

Statement

```
print("Hello", end = " ")
print("World")
```

Output

```
Hello World
```

Statement

```
print("Welcome", end = "~~~~")
print("Home")
```

Output

```
Welcome~~~~Home
```

Statement

```
print("In Python's embrace", end = ",\n")
print"\tElegance flows through whitespace", end = ",\n")
print("\t\tCode sings with grace", end = ".")
```

Output

```
In Python's embrace,
   Elegance flows through whitespace,
      Code sings with grace.
```

As our programs become more complex, we will need some way to make notes within our programs. We call this writing comments. To do this we start the commented line with a hash symbol (#). This tells Python that the line is not code, but rather a comment for the people who are reading the code. Comments can be on their own lines, or they can be written after a statement. Comments are essential for making code easier to understand, for both ourselves and other programmers who may read out the code later.

```
print("This is code")
#This is not code
```

For example:

```
#This is a haiku about Python
print("In Python's embrace", end = ",\n") #here I am using
end to insert a comma and a hard return
print"\tElegance flows through whitespace", end = ",\n")
#\t is a tab space
print("\t\tCode sings with grace", end = ".")
# I hope you enjoyed my haiku
```

Would output:

```
In Python's embrace,
    Elegance flows through whitespace,
        Code sings with grace.
```

The interpreter ignores the comments, but they help us make sense of complex code. Comments provide a way to document our thought process and clarify the purpose of certain parts of our code. Well commented code is easier to debug and is more maintainable over time.

We can also "comment out" a line of code instead of deleting it by adding a hash in front of it. This lets us temporarily remove a line without deleting it. This is useful when we are trying to make changes to a program but we are not quite sure if we will keep the changes or not.

Print statements with a "commented out" line

```
print("Once upon a time, in a land far, far, away...")
# print ("Dragons roared and wizards cast spells,")
print("A brave knight embarked on a daring quest.")
print("With sword in hand and armor gleaming.")
```

If we wanted to add the line about dragons back into our program, we would simply need to remove the hash. This is easier than having to rewrite the entire line, especially if some time has passed since we originally wrote it.

Unlike many programming languages, Python doesn't have a specific syntax for multiline comments. If you want to include comments that span multiple lines you have two opinions. The first is to simply put a hash in front of every line.

```
#This is a multiline comment
#It is useful for explaining complex sections of code
#It could also be used to remove a block of code
```

Really this is just a series of single line comments, but the overall purpose is the same.

The other opinion is technically not a comment, but since it has no impact on the overall program, the effect is the same. When we wrap a block of text in three quotation marks, it is called a string literal. String literals can cover multiple lines, giving us a convenient way to write multiline comments.

```
"""
This is also a multiline comment
Well actually it is a string literal
It can also be used to comment out a block of code
"""
```

While both methods work, using a series of single line comments is preferred. Triple quotes are often used in Python for a specific type of documentation called a docstring. We will discuss these later in Chapter 4.

2.2 Data Types

So far, we have looked at one data type in Python; the string. As discussed earlier, strings are sequences of characters enclosed within quotes. The string type is abbreviated to "str". Other common data types are *integers, floats,* and *Booleans*. There are other types that we will look at later in the book as well including *lists, tuples,* and *dictionaries*.

- Integers, or "int", are numerical values without decimal points. These can be positive or negative and are not written with quotation marks. Strings are the only data type that contains values surrounded by quotes.

- Floats, or "float" on the other hand are values that contain decimal places. These must contain decimal places. In some programming languages, it is extremely important to keep track of whether values are ints or floats, but it is only important in Python in some cases which we will explore later.

- Boolean values, or "bool" are considered truth values and are represented by True or False. These keywords must begin with a capital letter and must not be surrounded by quotes.

If we need to determine the type of a variable, we can use the `type()` function. If we write a program that uses `type()` on its own nothing will happen. We need to print the result of the `type()` function.

Printing types

```
Commands
print(type("Hello World"))
print(type(15))
print(type("15"))
print(type(4.5))
print(type("True"))
print(type(False))

Output
<class 'str'>
<class 'int'>
<class 'str'>
<class 'float'>
<class 'str'>
<class 'bool'>
```

In the code above, we can see much of what we would expect. "Hello World" is a string since it is a series of characters surrounded by quotation marks. 15 is an int since it is a numerical value with no quotations, but "15" is a string. 4.5 is a float due to the decimal. "True" looks like a Boolean, but the quotes make it a string. False is a Boolean.

The output from `type()` can be puzzling to some beginners in Python due to the use of the word "class" and also the angle brackets (< >). We will revisit this when we learn about object oriented programming in Chapter 6.

Python can sometimes be forgiving with data types and will automatically convert types when needed, assuming it is possible. This is known as an implicit type conversion. We often see this happen when we perform mathematical operations. If we try to add an integer and a float, for example 3.5 + 12, the integer will automatically be converted to a float without the need of code giving us the result of 15.5, a float, without *error*.

There are many other times when we may wish to perform an explicit type conversion. There are built-in functions for the main data types such as int(), float(), str(), and bool() which attempt to turn the argument into the specified data type, integer, float, string, and Boolean respectively. Be warned however, this is when you will likely see unexpected results or possibly errors. Not all values can be changed into other data types. It would be simple to understand that the string "15.8" can be turned into the float 15.8, or that the integer 3 can be turned into the string "3", but how could we change the float -13.5 into an integer? Instead of rounding, the decimal part is simply removed, giving us the value -13. Likewise, converting False to an integer, gives us the number 0. In Python, as in most programming languages, 0 is false and 1 is true.

Errors tend to occur when trying to convert strings to numerical values. If the string is not written like a number, there will be a *ValueError*, since the value is not appropriate for the function. We will look more into errors in Chapter 6.

A value error

Commands

```
print(int("Hello"))
```

Output

```
Traceback (most recent call last):
  File "<string>", line 1, in <module>
ValueError: invalid literal for int() with base 10: 'Hello'
```

Python errors can look complicated at first, but they reveal a lot of information that can help us identify problems. In this case, we can see the line number 1, and the statement that caused the error, print(int("Hello")). We also get a description of the error. In this case "Hello" cannot be represented as a number. Python specifies base 10 which are the numbers we deal with in our daily lives.

Fun Fact

Binary numbers are base 2. Since we have 10 fingers it makes sense for humans to use base 10 numbers, but computers can only count by looking at values of 0 or 1, off or on. It would be like counting on your fingers if you only had 2 fingers.

Luckily for us, working with data types in Python is fairly straightforward, but it can cause some issues from time to time. We will see a common issue in the next section.

2.3 Working with Variables

Computer programs would be fairly useless without user input. The simplest tool at our disposal is the keyboard. To get input from the keyboard, we can use the input function. Referencing the official documentation, we can see the syntax is simply input(prompt).

The `input()` function takes a string as an argument to prompt the user as to what they are meant to write as the input. For example, if we wanted to get a user's name, we could say `input ("What is your name? ")`. This will display "What is your name?" on the screen, as seen in the code below.

Input prompt

Commands

```
input("What is your name?")
```

Output

```
What is your name?
```

There are two things to keep in mind when using input. The input function doesn't add a space between the prompt and the cursor, so we often add a space or a colon at the end to make things more visually pleasing. The other is that while the input function returns the string entered by the user, it doesn't get stored anywhere by default. We need to store it in a *variable*.

Variables can be seen as places to store information. They can store any data type, but for now we will store strings in them. Variables should be named like functions. That is they should be lowercase and if they require multiple words, they should be separated by underscores. While we can use single letter variable names, it is better to be descriptive to make it easier to understand the code that we have written.

The code below shows a program that asks for a user's name and then prints out a customized welcome message.

Storing and printing variables

Commands

```
name = input("What is your name? ")
print("Hello", name)
```

Output

```
What is your name? Shawn
Hello Shawn
```

Note that the variable, name, is not wrapped in quotation marks. This is how Python understands the difference between the string name, and the variable name.

Variables versus strings

Statement
```
name = "Jimmy"
print("Hello", name)
```

Output
```
Hello Jimmy
```

Statement
```
name = "Jimmy"
print("Hello", "name")
```

Output
```
Hello name
```

With the ability to input and output information, we can begin to make simple programs. Here is an example that would ask a user for their favorite color and acknowledge the choice.

```
# This program prompts the user to enter their favorite
color
# and prints a message acknowledging their input.
# Prompt the user to enter their favorite color
color = input("Please enter your favorite color: ")

# Print a message acknowledging the user's input
print("Your favorite color is",color,". That's a great
choice!")
```

We have seen how to store the results of an input function into a variable as a string. We can also set the values of variables directly, a process called hard coding the values.

```
name = "Sarah"
age = "25"

print(name, "is", age)
```

This example will output "Sarah is 25". While this is not a very practical example, it does show us how to hard code values.

Variables in Python are *mutable*, meaning their values can be changed throughout the program. You can reassign a variable's value at any point, but doing so will overwrite its previous value: Python is also a dynamically typed language, so not only can we change the value of a variable, but we can also change the type.

```
age = 25
age = "fifty"
print(age)
```

Here the variable age starts as an integer value of 25 and is then overwritten to the string value "fifty". When printed, the string "fifty" is displayed.

For numerical values, we will often want to change their values mathematically. For example, we may want to increase, or *increment*, a value or decrease, or *decrement*, a value. There are two main ways to accomplish this.

Verbose

```
bank_balance = 500

#withdraw $20
bank_balance  = bank_balance - 20

#deposit $100
bank_balance = bank_balance + 100

print("Your balance is", bank_balance)
```

Shorthand

```
bank_balance = 500

#withdraw $20
bank_balance  -= 20

#deposit $100
bank_balance += 100

print("Your balance is", bank_balance)
```

Both of these will output "Your balance is 580" and both are valid, however the shorthand version is used by most programmers as it can change the value and reassign it without having to type the variable name twice. Table 2.1 shows some common shorthand mathematical reassignment operators.

Table 2.1   Shorthand for mathematically changing variables

Symbol	Meaning
+=	Add and reassign
-=	Subtract and reassign
*=	Multiply and reassign
/=	Divide and reassign

Understanding how variables work in Python is fundamental to writing effective and efficient code. They provide a way to store and manipulate data, enabling programmers to create dynamic and flexible applications.

2.4 Conditional Statements

Decisions are an important part of both everyday life and computer programming. If it is cold out you might choose to wear a jacket, otherwise a t-shirt might be fine. If you are hungry, you might grab a quick snack. In Python we use three keywords, if, else if; shortened to elif, and else. These statements can be used to make more dynamic programs that respond to different events.

Since we know a little about the basics of programming, we can start using some more practical examples. Many concerts have early bird tickets. If you buy before a certain date you get a discounted rate. A *flowchart* to represent a program to determine how much your concert tickets would cost could look like this.

Figure 2.2 **Pseudocode for ticket discounts**

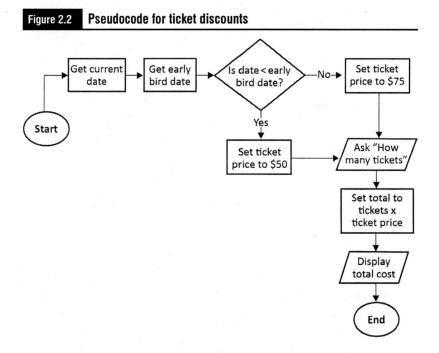

Focusing only on the decision piece, we would write the following code.

```
if date <= early_bird:
    ticket_price = 50
else:
    ticket_price = 75
```

The `if` keyword is followed by a conditional statement which ends with a colon. If the conditional statement is true, or more accurately True, then the associated code block is executed.

It is common to use the mathematical operators, as seen in Table 2.2, to compare values. Here we are checking if the date is less than or equal to the early bird date. The indented sections show the code blocks associated with each decision. The ticket price is only set to 50 if the date is less than or equal to the early bird date. The else statement tells us what to do if the if statement is not true. In this case the ticket price is set to 75.

Table 2.2   Comparison symbols

Symbol	Meaning
>	Greater than
>=	Greater than or equal to
<	Less than
<=	Less than or equal to
==	Equal to
!=	Not equal to

`Else` statements are a great way to catch any additional situations, but are not always required. For example, we could set our ticket price and apply a discount if it is before the early bird date.

```
ticket_price = 75
if date <= early_bird:
    ticket_price -= 25
```

Since we only need to modify the price if the early bird date hasn't passed, we no longer need the `else` statement here. Neither method is intrinsically better. Note the use of "−=" to decrement the value of ticket_price by 25.

For more complex situations, we can use a number of `else if` statements, which are written as `elif`. These let us write more blocks of code for more specific situations.

If you were traveling to a country that used Celsius instead of Fahrenheit it might be difficult to understand the temperature. We could write a quick program to see if the current temperature in Celsius is hot or cold. In this example, we have hard coded the value of 20ºC for the temperature.

A program to help understand Celsius

```
Commands
temp = 20

if temp > 30:
    print("It is hot outside")
elif temp > 15:
    print("It is nice outside")
elif temp > 0:
    print("It is cold outside")
else:
    print("It is freezing outside")

fahrenheit = (temp * 9/5) + 32
print("The temperature in Fahrenheit is", fahrenheit, "°F")
```

```
Output
It is nice outside
The temperature in Fahrenheit is 68.0 °F
```

When writing `if` statements in this way it is important to understand that the *conditions* are checked one at a time and once a statement is true, that code block is run and the others are not checked. Once we reach a line that is not indented, other than an `elif` or `else`, Python understands that we are done with the `if` statement.

In this code snippet, we set the value of `temp` to 20. First, we check if `temp` is greater than 30, it is not so we skip over the indented code and move onto the first `elif` statement. We check if the `temp` is greater than 15, which it is, so we run the indented code. We then ignore everything else until after the code block and resume the code on line 12. This performs the mathematics required to convert the Celsius temperature into Fahrenheit and then the result is printed to the screen.

Logical operators, such as "and", "or", and "not" can be used to give us more control over our conditional statements. Table 2.3 shows how these operators work to yield True or False.

Table 2.3	A logical truth table				
a	b	a and b	a or b	not a	not b
True	True	True	True	False	False
True	False	False	True	False	True
False	True	False	True	True	False
False	False	False	False	True	False

In the following snippet, we can see that the username has to be "admin" and the password "correctPassword" has to be entered. If either one is False, then the conditional statement is False and the welcome message is not displayed.

```
if username == "admin" and password == "correctPassword":
    print("Welcome, admin!")
```

In this snippet, we are checking if the age of the person is less than 5 or greater than 65. If the person is 4, for example the first part of the statement, age < 5, is True, but the second part, age > 65 is False. Unlike the "and" keyword, "or" only needs one of them to be True for the conditional statement to be True: If both conditions happen to be true, which cannot happen in this example, the condition will still be True.

```
if age < 5 or age > 65:
    print("You are eligible for a discount")
```

If statements can also be nested. This means that if statements can also have other if statements within them. While there is no actual limit to the number of if statements that can be nested, the more nesting we use, the more difficult it will be to read and understand the code. Nesting is a powerful technique, but it should not be overused, especially when "and" or "or" can be utilized. Just as ceramic figures feature intricate layers and designs, nested statements in Python create complex logic by layering conditional statements.

Figure 2.3   **Ceramic figurines**

Photo by Didssph, published February 22, 2021, Unsplash https://unsplash.com/
photos/red-blue-and-yellow-ceramic-figurine-PB80D_B4g7c

Consider a company that wants to use software to prescreen applicants for a job. They may want to check the applicant's qualifications first before checking any additional information.

Nested `if` statements

```
if qualified:
    if experience >=5:
        print("You have been added to the shortlist")
    else:
        print("You need more experience")
else:
    print("You are not qualified for this position")
```

Here if qualified is set to True then we enter the code block that contains the second `if` statement. In that statement, we check to see if the experience is set higher than or equal to 5. If so we shortlist the applicant. Even though this is a simple example, it is easy to see how nesting can get complicated if we were to continue nesting more and more if statements. Wherever possible, try to find ways to rewrite nested `if` statements into single `if` statements using logical operators. This makes the coding logic easier to follow and understand.

Avoiding nesting

```
if qualified and experience >=5:
    print("You have been added to the shortlist")
elif:
    print("You need more experience")
else:
    print("You are not qualified for this position")
```

2.5 Loops and Iteration

If we give someone a set of instructions to follow, it is likely that we will tell them to repeat certain steps. *Loops* are used in programming for this task. If we were changing the tires on a car, we would want to repeat the instructions for each tire, or in other words, we would want to do the set of instructions for each tire. In Python, we call this a *for-loop*. On the other hand, if we were using a jack to lift the vehicle we wouldn't necessarily know how many times we would need to pump the handle. We would want to repeat until the car was high enough. In Python, this is called a *while-loop*.

For-loops are used to loop a set number of times, often over each item in a sequence. Consider the following instructions for making chocolate chip cookies.

Combine dry ingredients

Add the first egg and mix well

Add the second egg and mix well

Add the third egg and mix well

Add chocolate chips and stir until dough forms

It is not hard to see how redundant the instructions are. Rather than explaining what to do with each egg specifically, we could just explain what to do with the eggs one at a time. This is the core concept of a for-loop.

As *pseudocode*, we could rewrite this as follows:

```
ADD dry ingredients to bowl
FOR all the eggs in the recipe:
    ADD egg to bowl
    MIX
ENDFOR
ADD chocolate chips
MIX
```

We will look at iterating over sequences further in Chapter 3, but for now we use `range()` alongside our for-loops. While it looks and acts like a function in many ways, `range()` is actually a special type of sequence that we can iterate over. There are two ways to create a range object: `range(stop)` or `range(start, stop, step=1)`[6]. In simple terms, if we supply one number, we are starting at zero and setting the stopping point, two numbers, we are setting the start and stopping points, and three numbers, we are setting the start and stopping points as well as how much we are changing by each time. We can use integers for these values, but trying to use a decimal value will cause an error. The stopping point is not included in the sequence.

6. Python Documentation, "Built-in Functions – Python 3.12.3 documentation accessed May 11, 2024, https://docs.python.org/3/library/functions.html

Example of ranges

Command	Sequence
range(5)	0,1,2,3,4
range(2,8)	2,3,4,5,6,7
range(2,8,2)	2,4,6
range(9,2,-1)	9,8,7,6,5,4,3
range(-3,5,2)	-3,-1,1,3

A for-loop starts with the keyword "for" followed by an iteration variable and the keyword is followed by a sequence. The statement ends with a colon and is followed by an indented code block to be run during each loop. It is a convention to use a lowercase "i" as the iteration variable but it is a better practice to use a more descriptive variable whenever possible. Consider the following example:

Hello and Goodbye

```
Commands
for i in range(3):
    print('Hello')
print('Goodbye')
```

```
Output
Hello
Hello
Hello
Goodbye
```

Here we are setting the variable i to each number in the sequence 0,1,2. We are not doing anything with this value, so there is no need to be overly descriptive. Sometimes programmers will use a single underscore (_) to indicate the variable is not being used but is required for the syntax. It is common to see the variables "i", "j", and "k" used by programmers, but whenever it is appropriate we should be using more descriptive variable names.

The range(3) gives us the sequence 0,1,2, so we run the indented block three times, once for each value of "i". Each time we print "Hello". Once the loop is complete, we execute the next unindented line and print "Goodbye"

So, if we were writing a countdown program, we might want to use:

```
for number in range(10,-1,-1):
    print(number)
print('Happy New Year')
```

If you were learning to play a new song on a guitar, you wouldn't know how many times you would need to practice, so a for-loop would not fit the situation. Instead you would want to use a while-loop. While-loops are used to loop while a condition is true and stop when the condition is false.

```
SET song to "Twinkle, Twinkle, Little Star"
WHILE learning song:
    PRACTICE
ENDWHILE
PLAY song
```

A for-loop wouldn't work here as we have no idea how long we will need to practice. The structure of a while-loop is different from a for-loop but is still similar. A while-loop uses the keyword "while" followed by a condition and ends with a colon. Like a for-loop, there follows an indented code block that is looped. There is a potential for running infinite loops when working with while-loops that we must keep in mind.

```
stuck = True
while stuck:
    print("I'm stuck")
print("I'm free")
```

This program, which we probably would not want to run, will forever print "I'm stuck". The value of stuck never gets changed to True, so the starting condition would never be False and the final line of code would never run.

While-loops are also not guaranteed to run. If the condition is not true when we reach the loop then the indented code block is skipped over completely. So, in this case only "I'm free" will print.

```
stuck = False
while stuck:
    print("I'm stuck")
print("I'm free")
```

A more practical example can be seen here.

```
playing = "yes"
while playing == "yes":
    print("This is fun")
    playing = input("Do you want to play some more? ")
print("We'll play some more later.")
```

Initially, we set the value of playing to "yes". This is important as it allows us to enter the loop since the value of playing is indeed equal to "yes". Next, we run the indented code, so we print "This is fun" and then get some input from the user which is reassigned to the value of playing. Once the indented code is complete, we return to the top of the code block and check if playing still equals "yes". If it is not, we exit the loop and print the final statement.

Many beginners get confused by the use of single equals (=) versus double equals (==). A single equals sign is used to assign a value to a variable, while a double equals sign checks to see if values are equal.

`playing = "yes"`	Assigns the value of "yes" to the variable playing.
`playing == "yes"`	Checks the value of the variable playing to see if it equals "yes"

It is common for beginning programmers to determine which type of loop is best, and it often comes down to preference. We might choose to perform the code block once for each item in the cart, which would be best suited to a for-loop. We would get the item's price and add it to our total. Once the code is run for each item, we exit the loop and output the total.

```
SET total to 0
FOR all the items in the cart:
    SET price to item price
    ADD price to total
ENDFOR
OUTPUT total
```

Using a while-loop, we would first check to see if there is anything in our cart. If there is, we would take the item out and then get its price and add it to the total. We would continue this process until there are no other items in the cart and then output the total.

```
SET total to 0
WHILE item in cart:
    REMOVE item from cart
    SET price to item price
    ADD price to total
ENDWHILE
OUTPUT total
```

To gain additional control of for-loops and while-loops we have two keywords that come in handy: break and continue.

Break, not surprisingly, breaks a loop at the point where it is executed. After breaking the loop the code block will not be run again even if the sequence is not complete or the condition is not false. In this code example, we will try to guess a number within three tries. There are multiple ways to do this, but we will use a for-loop to repeat the guessing code three times and break the loop if the guess is correct.

```python
my_number = "5"
print("I am thinking of a number between 1 and 10")
for guess in range(3):
    your_number = input("What is your guess? ")
    if your_number == my_number:
        print("You got it!")
        break
    else:
        print("Nope!")
```

Here, if the values of your_number and my_number are equal, we do not want to keep running the loop, so we use break to exit the loop.

Continue is a little trickier to understand as it restarts the loop without finishing the rest of the code in the loop. In essence, we skip the remaining code and continue from the top. In this example, a superstitious builder has avoided labeling any floor as floor 13 so that floor 14 is directly above floor 12.

Commands

```
for floor in range(10,15):
    if floor == 13:
        continue
    print("Welcome to floor", floor)
```

Output

```
Welcome to floor 10
Welcome to floor 11
Welcome to floor 12
Welcome to floor 14
Welcome to floor 15
```

Since our sequence goes 10,11,12,13,14 and we do not want to include 13, we can check the floor, and if it equals 13 we can continue without executing the print statement. This does not break the loop but instead skips the printing of the floor number.

Much like we nested `if` statements, we can also nest loops. Like `if` statements, nesting loops can be done when necessary but can complicate the reading of code and should be used sparingly. When we start looking into lists of lists in Chapter 3, nesting becomes unavoidable.

Here we can see a classic childhood "knock knock" joke recreated in code. We are using a for-loop to control how many times we complete the "orange" part of the joke and inside of that for-loop, we have while-loops that run until the correct response is given. The indentation is required by Python, but it also makes it easier to see exactly what is repeated as part of the for-loop and what specifically belongs to the while-loops inside of for-loops.

```
for i in range(2):
    print("Knock knock")
    response = ""
    while response != "who's there?":
        response = input('-')
    print("Orange")
    while response != "orange who?":
        response = input('-')

print("Knock knock")
response = ""
while response != "who's there?":
    response = input('-')
print("Banana")
while response != "banana who?":
    response = input('-')
print("Orange you glad I didn't say banana?")
```

A less fun but more practical example is creating a times table chart. We start with num1 at 1 and then complete the sequence for num2 going from 1 to 5. When we finish with num2, we print a blank line and then increase num1 by 1. num2 goes from 1 to 5 again and we continue until num1 gets to 5.

Commands

```
for num1 in range(1,6):
    for num2 in range(1,6):
        print(num1*num2, end ='\t')
    print()
```

Output

```
1   2    3    4    5
2   4    6    8    10
3   6    9    12   15
4   8    12   16   20
5   10   15   20   25
```

When we begin programming it is important to realize that the code we write may not be the most efficient and may not follow all of the best practices of writing code, however we need to be aware that there are bad habits that budding programmers can easily fall into. While there is nothing wrong with nesting, there are often more efficient ways of writing our code.

In the next chapter, we will look into some of the common data structures available in Python, while continuing to build upon the foundational knowledge from this chapter. This will allow us to build more complex and practical programs to solve practical problems.

Quiz

1. **Why is the hash (#) used before certain lines in Python?**
   a. To execute specific lines of code
   b. To indicate unsaved edits
   c. To mark errors in the code
   d. To provide comments for people reading the code

2. **What would be the output of print ("Hello", "World", sep = "-")?**
   a. Hello World
   b. Hello
      World
   c. Hello-World
   d. HelloWorld

3. **What does the optional argument "end" do in the `print()` function?**
   a. It determines how arguments are separated
   b. It immediately ends and executes the statement
   c. It sets the character printed at the end of the output
   d. It sets the maximum width of the output before it ends

4. **What is an optional argument?**
   a. An argument that determines if values are returned
   b. An argument that has a default value
   c. An argument that is always specified
   d. An argument that is not defined

5. **Which data type would "Hello" represent?**

   a. Boolean

   b. Float

   c. Integer

   d. String

6. **Which data type would be used to represent a number without decimal points?**

   a. Boolean

   b. Float

   c. Integer

   d. String

7. **What is the purpose of the `int()` function?**

   a. Checks to see if a value is an integer

   b. Converts a value to an integer, if possible

   c. Iterates over a sequence

   d. Takes numerical input

8. **What happens when we try to convert the float -2.85 into an integer?**

   a. The decimal is removed, making it -2

   b. The value is made positive, making it 2.85

   c. The value is rounded, making it -3

   d. There will be an error

9. **When using `input()`, what type of value is returned?**

   a. Boolean

   b. Integer

   c. String

   d. It depends on the information entered

10. **Which statement would get integer input from the user?**

    a. tickets = input("How many tickets do you need? ")

    b. tickets = int(input("How many tickets do you need? "))

    c. tickets = input(int("How many tickets do you need? "))

    d. tickets = input("How many tickets do you need? ", int)

Answers	1 – d	2 – c	3 – c	4 – b	5 – d
	6 – c	7 – b	8 –a	9 – c	10 – b

Chapter Summary

◆ Programming languages have their own syntax that has to be followed to write programs.

◆ Variables are useful for storing information in a variety of data types.

◆ Conditional logic can be used to write programs that branch, making them more dynamic.

◆ For-loops and while-loops can be used to repeat blocks of code, making code more compact and readable.

Chapter **3**

Data Structures in Python

This chapter covers the data structures available in Python. We will explore how lists, tuples, sets, and dictionaries can be used to help us write more complex code without having to create an endless stream of variables to keep track of everything. Data structures help us keep related material together and give us a way of accessing data in a simplified manner

The key learning objectives of this chapter are:

- Understand the differences between lists, tuples, sets, and dictionaries.

- Create and modify the various data structures.

- Use methods associated with various data structures.

- Handling errors associated with accessing and modifying data structures

3.1 Introduction to Data Structures

In the last chapter, we explored many key features of *Python* including *variables*. Variables are like containers that hold values such as *strings, integers, floats,* and *Booleans*. Python has several useful *data structures* that can allow us to organize our data in much more efficient ways. The four *data structures* that we will focus on in this chapter are *lists, tuples, sets,* and *dictionaries*. These data structures can be stored inside of variables just like other data. Understanding these structures will allow us to create more advanced and dynamic programs.

Which data structure we use depends on what we need to do within our program. We will go into each in more detail as we go through this chapter, but we will start with a brief comparison of each. Lists are ordered collections of items that can be changed throughout our programs. As with variables, lists are *mutable*. A simple grocery list is a good real-life example of a list. Once we write a grocery list, we are free to add or remove items as we see fit. We might reorder the list, or we could split it into smaller lists if we wanted to spend less time in the store at one time. Lists are excellent to use when we need an ordered collection of items that might need to change. Tuples on the other hand are like lists in that they are ordered collections, but they are *immutable*, meaning that once they are created they cannot be changed. A fixed set of GPS coordinates of major cities could be an example of a tuple as the cities and their latitude and longitude would not change. Many novice programmers use lists more than tuples since they can be modified, but there are many advantages to tuples that we will get into later. Tuples work best for fixed data sets that will never change.

Sets are unordered collections of unique items, which are mutable. If we wanted to hold a prize draw, we might put everyone's name in a hat. We wouldn't want to have anyone's name in more than once, and we wouldn't want to know the order ahead of time as that would remove any randomness to the draw. There are also many unique operations which we perform on sets which we will explore later. Sets are best used when we need a unique collection of items. Dictionaries are a complex, but useful data structure. They are a collection of information stored based on key values. A dictionary in Python is much like a dictionary in real life, where we look up the definition of a word by looking it up. Unlike a real dictionary, a dictionary in Python can store any number of types of data. For example, your phone's contact list could be considered a dictionary. The phone numbers are attached to the names of people that you know. We call this a *key-value pair*, where the value is the stored information, a phone number in this case, and the key is what it is stored under, in this case a name. Dictionaries are an extremely useful data structure that are essential to master and are most useful when we need to associate pairs of items.

Since we haven't started working with these data structures yet it may be tricky to understand why we might need to use these structures since we already use variables as containers. The easiest answer is that we would quickly end up with very bloated code with a huge number of variable names storing very similar data. If we wanted to store the contact names of three people, we could easily write a simple program with three variables.

```
person1 = "Jimmy"
person2 = "Sarah"
person3 = "Omar"
```

You can imagine however how quickly this would grow if we were building a contact list application for a large business! As well, we are only storing the names at this point. We may want their numbers, job titles, positions, and more. All of which would have to be stored in their own variables. As well these data structures allow us to access data quickly without having to remember which variables contain which information. Data structures come with *methods* that allow us to quickly search for the information that we need. They are also optimized to save memory and perform operations quickly and efficiently.

3.2 Working with Lists and Tuples

Lists and tuples have many similarities and can be easily confused by beginners. We already discussed how lists are mutable and tuples are immutable, so when we want to deal with information that may change it is best for us to use lists. Static information can be more efficiently stored in tuples

3.2.1 Lists

In Python we create lists by using square brackets. We can start by creating an empty list, or we can populate it with some initial data. The information can be of any type and we can mix data types within the list.

```
empty_list = []
filled_list = ["apple", "banana","orange"]
mixed_list = ["apple", 7, 8.5, True]
```

Since lists are mutable, we need to know how to add data to our list. To do so, we can use the .append() method or the

.insert() method. We call these methods instead of *functions* because they act on the specific list that we are using. They are written with a dot after the list name. The .append() method takes the value we want to add and puts it at the end of the list. The .append() method modifies the list in place, meaning that we are changing the list directly and do not need to reassign it to the variable.

For example in:

```
employees = ["Olivia", "James"]
employees.append("Emily")
```

The list stored in the variable employees is now ["Olivia", "James", "Emily"]

The insert() method allows us to insert a new value at a specific *index,* or location, within the list. .insert() has the *syntax* .insert(index, value). It is important to note that Python, as well as most programming languages, uses zero indexing, meaning that the first item in the list is at index 0, with the next at index 1.

If we wanted to place a new employee, Michael, as the second item in the list (index 1), we would write:

```
employees.insert(1, "Michael")
```

Our employees' list would now be ["Olivia", "Michael", "James", "Emily"].

Also useful is removing data. Values can be removed from lists by either the location or by the value itself. These can both produce *errors* if we are not careful. If we want to remove James from our employee list, we can simply write:

```
employees.remove("James")
```

This will change our employees list to ["Olivia", "Michael", "Emily"]. This modifies the list in place meaning that the list changes under the current variable name and does not need to be reassigned.

There are two potential issues that can arise from using the .remove() method. The first issue is if the value is not in the list, there will be a ValueError and the program will stop running. Luckily, Python has an "in" keyword that can be used to check if a value is contained within a list. So before trying to remove James from the employee list, we can check if James is even in the list of employees. We will use an if *statement* like in the previous chapter.

```
if "James" in employees:
    employees.remove("James")
```

This first checks if there is a James in the employees list and then removes it only if there is. This way we can avoid the potential error. We will look more at error handling in later chapters.

The second issue is that, remove() only removes the first occurrence of a value in a list so if we had two James in our list, only the first would be removed. Depending on the needs of our program this might be fine, however let's look at how we could address these issues in our code.

Imagine we were in charge of a large mall and we received word that Moonlight Market was going bankrupt. Now we need to remove all Moonlight Markets from our mall. The following *flowchart* shows our process. Once we have the list of stores, we check if "Moonlight Market" is in our store list. If not, we don't need to do anything. If it is in the list, we remove it. Since a large mall could have more than one of the same stores, we will need to check again and repeat until there is no "Moonlight Market" in our list. Since we do not know how many times we will need to repeat this process, we will be using a *while-loop*.

Figure 3.1   Flowchart for removing from a list without error

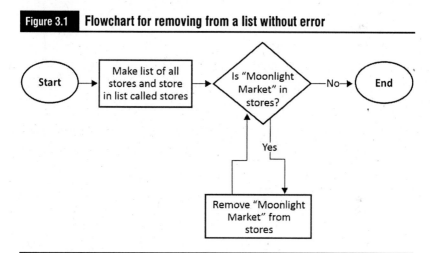

```
stores = ["Sunrise Books","Moonlight Market",
          "Gadget Shop","Magic Chest",
          "Moonlight Market"]
while "Moonlight Market" in stores:
    stores.remove("Moonlight Market")
print(stores)
```

The above code will output ['Sunrise Books', 'Gadget Shop', 'Magic Chest'] since the two Moonlight Markets were removed.

To access an item of the list, we can use the index of the item, again remembering that lists are indexed from zero. Table 3.1 shows the values of a list using indexing.

Table 3.1	**Accessing list items by index**

shopping_list = ["bread", "milk", "eggs"]	
Input	Output
print(shopping_list[0])	"bread"
print(shopping_list[1])	"milk"
print(shopping_list[2])	"eggs"

Items can also be indexed by negative values. -1 is the last index while -2 is the second last index and so on. If you try to access an index that does not exist, whether positive or negative, you will get an *IndexError*. If we had a list of all of the States in the US in alphabetical order and we tried to access the 51st item in the list we would get an error since there would only be 50 items in the list. To help with this issue, we can use the len() function to get the length of a list but we must be careful. The length of a list is just how many items are in the list, so len(states) would equal 50. Trying to access states[50] would give an error because index 50 is actually the 51st item in the list.

Figure 3.2 A map of the United States

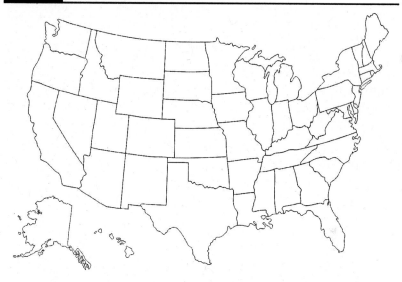

Photo by Freepik, published on March 31, 2022, https://www.freepik.com/premium-vector/hand-drawn-usa-outline-map-illustration_25206874.htm#from_view=detail_alsolike

For simplicity, we will only look at 10 ten states in this example but this could easily be extended.

```python
# List of some U.S. states in alphabetical order
states = ["Alabama", "Alaska", "Arizona", "Arkansas",
   "California", "Colorado", "Connecticut",
   "Delaware", "Florida", "Georgia"]
list_length = len(states)
index = int(input( "Enter the index of the state: "))
if index < list_length and index >= -list_length:
   print("The state at index", index, "is", states[index])
else:
   print(user_index, "is an invalid index")
```

In this example we make sure the user enters a value less than the length of the list to ensure there is a value present before trying to access it. We also need to ensure the value is greater than or equal to the negative length of the list, as we can also access list items counting from the back. Checking these conditions allows us to avoid errors which would stop our program.

In the last chapter, we looked at using *for-loops* to *loop* through a sequence. While we initially used `range()` to create a sequence, but we can also loop through a list directly. There is no new syntax here. We simply put the variable the list is stored within, or a new list, instead of the `range()` function.

If we had a list of business expenses over a week, we could loop through and get a total of expenses for the week as follows.

Commands

```
business_expenses = [100,75,30,100,30,17,28]
total = 0
for expense in business_expenses:
    total += expense
print("The weekly expenses are",total)
```

Output

```
The weekly expenses are 380
```

In this example we take each value in the list in sequence and store it under the variable expense. We then add the expense to the total. One benefit to this approach is that the code would not have to be rewritten for different lengths of data. We could use the same code for a week, a month, or a year of data. Writing code that can be reused is a very useful skill to develop.

Sometimes we want to keep track of the index that we are on during our loop. In our business expense example we might want to print out the expenses for each day. Many novice programmers will use the range function to meet this goal as follows.

Commands

```
business_expenses = [100,75,30,100,30,17,28]
total = 0
for day in range(len(business_expenses)):
    expense = business_expenses[day]
    print("Day", day+1, "expenses are", expense)
    total += expense
print("The weekly expenses are",total)
```

Output

```
Day 1 expenses are 100
Day 2 expenses are 75
Day 3 expenses are 30
Day 4 expenses are 100
Day 5 expenses are 30
Day 6 expenses are 17
Day 7 expenses are 28
The weekly expenses are 380
```

Here we use `range()` to make the sequence 0,1,2,3,4,5,6 and use these one at a time to access the expense at that index. We print "day + 1" since computers count from 0 but humans count from 1. There are times where this approach can be useful, but a more elegant option is to use the `enumerate` function. Enumerate is used to track the number of values that we have looped over and has the syntax `enumerate(iterable, start=0)` where `iterable` is our list, or another data type that we can loop over, and `start` is an optional value that we can set if we don't want to start at zero.[7] When we use `enumerate` we need two variables for our for-loop. The first variable tracks the count and the second tracks the value. We can revise our example as follows.

---

7. Python Documentation, "Built-in Functions – Python 3.12.3 documentation" accessed May 22, 2024, https://docs.python.org/3/library/functions.html

Commands

```
business_expenses = [100,75,30,100,30,17,28]
total = 0
for day, expense in enumerate(business_expenses, 1):
    print("The expenses for day", day, "are", expense)
    total += expense
print("The weekly expenses are",total)
```

Output

```
The expenses for day 1 are 100
The expenses for day 2 are 75
The expenses for day 3 are 30
The expenses for day 4 are 100
The expenses for day 5 are 30
The expenses for day 6 are 17
The expenses for day 7 are 28
The weekly expenses are 380
```

This approach is much more streamlined as we can specify that we are counting from 1 for the days, so we no longer need to add. We use the variable day to count the number of values we have looped over and store their value in the variable expense. This is a somewhat advanced technique but it allows for more readable code.

3.2.2 Tuples

Tuples are basically immutable lists and share many similarities with them. Tuples are mostly used for representing fixed collections of values. Creating a tuple is similar to creating a list, but instead of using square brackets we use round brackets. Like lists, you can create an empty tuple, but this would be pointless since we cannot edit it later, so we will want to populate tuples when we create them. Tuples are ordered collections and the indexing works identically to lists.

A simple example:

```python
my_tuple = ('apple', 'banana', 'cherry')
first_item = my_tuple[0]
last_item = my_tuple[-1]
print(first_item, last_item)
```

This would print out "apple cherry".

Looping over tuples is also identical to lists, so we could have written our business expense example with a tuple and there would be no difference to the output.

Commands

```python
business_expenses = (100,75,30,100,30,17,28)
total = 0
for day, expense in enumerate(business_expenses, 1):
    print("The expenses for day", day, "are", expense)
    total += expense
print("The weekly expenses are",total)
```

Output

```
The expenses for day 1 are 100
The expenses for day 2 are 75
The expenses for day 3 are 30
The expenses for day 4 are 100
The expenses for day 5 are 30
The expenses for day 6 are 17
The expenses for day 7 are 28
The weekly expenses are 380
```

Literally the only difference to the code is the rounded brackets to let Python know to store the information as a tuple.

So, if tuples can do less than lists, why would we ever want to use tuples? Since tuples are immutable they can never be changed. This is both a blessing and a curse. Once we set the values in a tuple, we have no way of changing them, which is a drawback, but on the other side, we know that we cannot accidentally change the value of the data later on. This makes tuples more secure than lists. *Programming* is not usually a solo activity and we need ways to indicate to other programmers on our teams that some values should not be modified. Tuples give an excellent way to do this.

Another fact that beginners often do not consider is memory usage. Since tuples are created all at once and do not require methods to modify them, they have a smaller footprint than lists. When they are created, they can be assigned a location within the system's memory where the data can all sit together and be quickly accessed. When a list is created, Python assigns extra memory so that it can be easily modified, but it takes up more space than needed. As a list grows and changes beyond this extra allocated space, some of the items may be located in different areas of the computer's memory. This means that not only does the new data need to be stored, but the new location of the data needs to be recorded as well.

In a simple sense, in a tuple, we know the location of the next item because it is right next to the previous entry. In a list the items could be scattered about so we need additional information about how to get to the next piece of information. This makes tuples more memory-efficient and faster to access in certain situations since there is less waste in modifying the structure or tracking changes in location.

This is not likely going to have much of an effect in the small programs we are writing at this point, but a nice rule of thumb is to only use lists when we intend to modify the data, and use tuples when the data will not be modified.

One last note before moving on, much like we have int(), float(), and str() to change the data type of values, we can also use list() and tuple() to change tuples to lists and lists to tuples.

3.3 Manipulating Sets and Dictionaries

3.3.1 Sets

Both lists and tuples are ordered collections of values, but there are times where we might want an unordered collection. Sets are useful for storing values that do not require a specific order. They also hold unique items, so the same entry cannot be stored twice. There are also special operations that we can perform on sets that we cannot directly perform on lists or tuples.

Creating a set is similar to creating a list or tuple, but they are surrounded by curly brackets. So a simple set would be created by:

```
my_set = {'apple', 'banana', 'cherry'}
```

Creating an empty set is slightly trickier because dictionaries also use curly brackets. When we create a set, Python can recognize that it is a set based on the structure of the information, however an empty set has no information to interpret. When Python sees an empty set of curly brackets, it assumes we are creating an empty dictionary. To create an empty set, we just write:

```
empty_set = set()
```

Just like lists, we have methods to change sets by adding and subtracting values, but the names are different. To add values to a set, we use the .add() method. Like with lists, the .add() method modifies the set in place.

```
my_set = {'apple', 'banana', 'cherry'}
my_set.add('watermelon')
print(my_set)
```

We would expect this to print out {'apple', 'banana', 'cherry', 'watermelon'}, but since sets are unordered we could get the information in any order, as seen in Table 3.2.

Table 3.2   Five sample outputs from printing a set

{'banana', 'cherry', 'apple', 'watermelon'}
{'cherry', 'apple', 'banana', 'watermelon'}
{'banana', 'cherry', 'watermelon', 'apple'}
{'watermelon', 'apple', 'banana', 'cherry'}
{'banana', 'watermelon', 'cherry', 'apple'}

If we try to add something that is already contained within the set, the set will remain unchanged and no error will occur. This is an absolutely amazing feature of sets in the right circumstances. Imagine a classroom setting where we wanted to make sure all of the students answered a question over the course of a day. Naturally some students may answer more than once, but we are only concerned with if they answered a question and not how many times they answered. If we used a list, we would have to check if the student was in the list and if not, we would have to then add them to the list. Using sets, we would just try to add the student to the set. If the student was already in the set, nothing would happen, but if not, they would be added. As seen in Figure 3.3, this occurs without any extra coding on our part.

Figure 3.3   Recording unique values in lists and sets

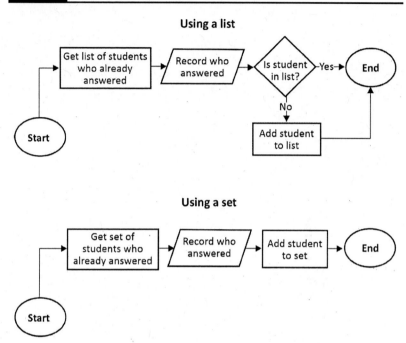

Removing values from a set can be done by one of two methods: `.remove()` and `.discard()`. Both operate in place and remove values from the set, but `.remove()` will cause an error if the value is not in the set. For now, it is recommended to just use `.discard()`, but once we get into error handling there may be times when `.remove()` is more appropriate.

Our classroom example could be reimagined to have a set of all the students in the class and to call the `.discard()` method every time a student answers a question. This will leave us with a set of all the students who have not answered questions. Since a set is a collection of values, we can use a for-loop to print out the names of students who have not yet answered questions.

Commands

```
students = {"Alice", "Bob", "Charlie", "David", "Eve", "Frank",
            "Grace"}
students.discard("Alice")
students.discard("Bob")
students.discard("Charlie")
students.discard("Zara")
# Zara was not in the set as she answered a question earlier
students.discard("Charlie")
# Charlie has already been removed, but there is no error
# Print out the remaining names in the set
print("Remaining students in the set:")
for student in students:
    print(student, "has yet to answer a question")
```

Output

```
Remaining students in the set:
Grace has yet to answer a question
Frank has yet to answer a question
David has yet to answer a question
Eve has yet to answer a question
```

The set still contains David, Eve, Frank, and Grace so they would each be assigned to the value of student and their message would be printed out. If the set was empty, no messages would be printed.

A lot of the power of sets comes from their ability to support operations like *union, intersection,* and *difference.* A union makes a new set that contains all of the elements in either set. We have two options to create a union. The first is to use the .union() method on a set, passing in the second set.

```
union_set = set1.union(set2)
```

The other option is to use the union operator, indicated by a "|", sometimes called a pipe.

```
union_set = set1 | set2
```

Both perform the same task, so it is really a matter of preference. The first option is a little more readable when reviewing code, but there is something elegant about the second.

If we were collecting hockey cards, we could use a union to create a set of all unique cards.

```python
pack1 = {"Wayne", "Mario", "Bobby", "Sidney"}
pack2 = {"Alex", "Sidney", "Patrick", "Bobby"}
all_cards = pack1.union(pack2)
print("Total card's collected:", all_cards)
```

This example would print out our total unique collection. Since sets are unordered, we cannot know which way they would print, but we would get something like "Total card's collected: {'Patrick', 'Sidney', 'Bobby', 'Mario', 'Wayne', 'Alex'}"

Like lists and tuples, we can loop over sets as well using the same context if we wanted to print out each item in the set.

```python
for cards in all_cards:
    print(card, "collected")
```

Intersections, from the `.intersection()` method or `&` operator, show the common values in two sets. This could be helpful when trying to come to a consensus between two people as to what to watch.

```python
your_shows = {
  "Galactic Quest", "Mystery Manor",
  "Dragon's Realm", "Future Frontiers"
  }
friend_shows = {
  "Future Frontiers", "Enchanted Forest",
  "Dragon's Realm", "Time Travelers"
  }
common_shows = your_shows.intersection(friend_shows)
print("Why don't you watch one of these?", common_shows)
```

Here we would get an output that includes the shows "Future Frontiers" and "Dragon's Realm", eliminating the need for endless streaming service scrolling.

The order of sets in union and intersection does not matter, but when it comes to difference it is important. Using `.difference()`, or simply "-", will create a set of values that is in the first set, but not the second. Consider if a company interviewed two highly skilled candidates for a programming job. It might be important to look at the skills each has over the other to help make a decision.

```
Commands
lila_skills = {
  "Python", "Data Analysis",
  "Project Management"
  }
jasmine_skills = {
  "Project Management", "Communication",
  "Python"
  }
lila_unique = lila_skills.difference(jasmine_skills)
jasmine_unique = jasmine_skills.difference(lila_skills)
print("Lila has the unique skills", lila_unique)
print("Jasmine has the unique skills", jasmine_unique)
```

```
Output
Lila has the unique skills {'Data Analysis'}
Jasmine has the unique skills {'Communication'}
```

Quickly, we can see that Lila has data analysis skills that Jasmine does not have, but Jasmine has extra communication skills. This may help the company reach a hiring decision faster.

Finally, like lists and tuples, we can use `set()` to transform a list or tuple into a set. This can be useful when we want to eliminate any duplicates in our lists and tuples, however it can be time consuming for large lists and tuples.

3.3.2 Dictionaries

Dictionaries are ordered collections of items stored as key-value pairs. The keys must be unique, but trying to reuse keys simply overwrites the value with no errors. In older versions of Python, dictionaries were unordered but that changed in Python 3.7.[8] Like sets, dictionaries are created using curly brackets. Python understands we are creating a dictionary and not a set since we use keys and values which are separated by a colon.

```
info_dict = {"Name":"Shawn", "Location":"New York"}
```

In the `info_dict` there are two key-value pairs. "Name" and "Location" are the keys and the associated values are "Shawn" and "New York". To access this data, we write the name of the dictionary followed by square brackets with the key inside. So `info_dict["Name"]` would give us "Shawn". We can add information to a dictionary in a similar manner.

In this example, we will start with an empty dictionary and add information to it. Empty dictionaries can be created by using curly brackets without any information. Here we are creating a dictionary of items for a yard sale as keys and their prices as values.

```
sale_items = {}
sale_items["chair"] = 50
sale_items["lamp"] = 25
sale_items["artwork"] = 200
sale_items["book"] = 10
print(sale_items)
```

Our dictionary now looks like this: {'chair': 50, 'lamp': 25, 'artwork': 200, 'book': 10}.

---

8. Floyd, K. (2020). Interpersonal communication. Ohio: McGraw-Hill Education, p. 53.

As the day goes by we will hopefully sell some items. To remove the items from the dictionary we can use the keyword `del` or the `.pop()` method. Using the keyword `del` removes the item from the dictionary in place, so we do not need to reassign the dictionary to a variable. To use `del` we use the syntax `del dictionary[key]`. To remove "book" from our dictionary we would use the line:

```
del sale_items["book"]
```

The `.pop()` method may be more useful in this case because not only does it delete the key-value pair, but it also returns the value. This could be useful in this case because we may want to save the price in a variable so that we can use it later.

```
price = sale_items.pop("book")
```

In both cases the dictionary is changed to {'chair': 50, 'lamp': 25, 'artwork': 200}, but using `.pop()` lets us store the price. Regardless of which method we choose to use, if the key does not exist, we will get a *KeyError*. To avoid this, we can employ a method similar to the one used for removing items from lists.

Figure 3.4   Safely removing items from dictionaries

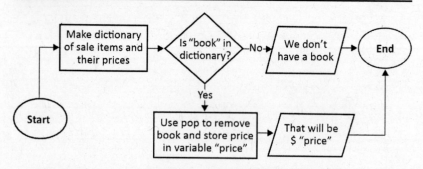

Figure 3.4 shows a flowchart for the following code.

Commands

```
sale_items = {
   'chair': 50, 'lamp': 25,
   'artwork': 200, 'book':10
   }
if "book" in sale_items:
   price = sale_items.pop("book")
   print("That will be $",price, sep = '')
   else:
print("We don't have a book")
```

Output

```
That will be $10
```

Looping over dictionaries is a bit more complex than other data structures and it really depends on what information we want to iterate over. There are three methods we can use: .keys(), .values(), and .items(). In keeping with our yard sale example, maybe we want to print out all the keys and values to display the items and their prices.

Commands

```
sale_items = {
   'chair': 50, 'lamp': 25,
   'artwork': 200, 'book': 10
   }
for item, price in sale_items.items():
   print(item, ": $",price, sep="")
```

Output

```
chair: $50
lamp: $25
artwork: $200
book: $10
```

We use both item and price since .items() will return a key and value together. The key is stored in item and the value is stored in price.

If we only wanted to list the items for sale and did not need the price as we go through the loop, we can just use the `.keys()` method.

Commands

```
sale_items = {'chair': 50, 'lamp': 25,
              'artwork': 200, 'book': 10}
print("The following items are for sale:")
for item in sale_items.keys():
    print(item)
```

Output

```
The following items are for sale:
chair
lamp
artwork
book
```

In this particular example, there is no reason to access the values without the keys, but if we wanted to we could have used the `.values()` method in the same manner as the `.keys()` method.

3.4 Overview

This exploration of lists, tuples, sets, and dictionaries really just scratches the surface of these data structures. There are many other methods available for each. More information can be found in the official Python documentations about other methods as well as advanced techniques such as list comprehension, dictionary comprehension, and nested data structures.[9] As we continue learning more about programming, understanding how and when to use these structures will become second nature. As a handy

9. Python Documentation, "Data Structures – Python 3.12.3 documentation", accessed May 24th, 2024, ttps://docs.python.org/3/tutorial/datastructures.html.

reference, Table 3.3 offers a comparison between these major data structures.

| Table 3.3 | Summary of Data Structures | | | |

Feature	List	Tuple	Set	Dictionary
Definition	Ordered, mutable collection	Ordered, immutable collection	Unordered collection of unique items	Ordered collection of key-value pairs
Syntax	`my_list = [1,2,3]`	`my_tuple = (1,2,3)`	`my_set = {1,2,3}`	`my_dict = {'item1':1, 'item2':2}`
Mutability	Mutable	Immutable	Mutable	Mutable
Order	Ordered	Ordered	Unordered	Ordered
Duplicate Values	Allowed	Allowed	Not allowed	Key cannot be duplicated
Accessing Values	By index	By index	Not directly	By key

In the next chapter, we will look into importing libraries to access more functions within Python and learn how to write our own functions. This will make our code more organized and reusable.

Quiz

1. **Which describes a list?**

   a. An unordered collection of items

   b. An ordered, mutable collection of items

   c. An immutable collection of items

   d. A collection of key-value pairs

2. **Which data structure is immutable?**

   a. Dictionary

   b. List

   c. Set

   d. Tuple

3. **Which data structure is represented by {"Answer1": "A", "Answer2": "B", "Answer3": "C"}?**

   a. Dictionary

   b. List

   c. Set

   d. Tuple

4. **If a programmer wanted a unique collection of values, what data structure would they use?**

   a. Dictionary

   b. List

   c. Set

   d. Tuple

5. **In the following code snippet, what would be printed to the console?**

   points = [6,3,8,10]

   print(points[3])

   a. 3

   b. 6

   c. 8

   d. 10

6. **If we wanted to add an item to the end of a list, which method would be used?**

   a. `add()`

   b. `append()`

   c. `insert()`

   d. `push()`

7. **A dictionary stored in the variable "person" is defined as {"name": "Harold", "age",23, "occupation": "student"}. Which statement would print "Harold" to the console?**

   a. `print(person[name])`

   b. `print(person["name"])`

   c. `print(person.get[name])`

   d. `print(person.get["name"])`

8. Given the code snippet, what would be printed to the console?

```
my_car = {'color': 'red', 'fuel': 25}
my_car['fuel'] = 20
print(my_dict)
```

   a. {'color': 'red', 'fuel': 25}

   b. {'color': 'red'}

   c. {'color': 'red', 'fuel': 20}

   d. {'fuel': 20}

9. How can you determine how many items are in a list called my_list?

   a. `len(my_list)`

   b. `my_list.count()`

   c. `my_list.length()`

   d. `my_list.items()`

10. What happens if we try to remove a key-value pair from a dictionary if the key does not exist?

   a. The dictionary is unchanged

   b. We get a value of -1 for the key

   c. We get an IndexError

   d. We get a KeyError

Answers	1 – b	2 – d	3 – a	4 – c	5 – d
	6 – b	7 – b	8 –c	9 – a	10 – d

Chapter Summary

◆ Python has several built-in data structures with their own characteristics and uses.

◆ Lists are ordered mutable collections that are indexed starting at zero.

◆ Tuples are ordered immutable collections that are indexed starting at zero.

◆ Sets are unordered mutable collections that have no order.

◆ Dictionaries are ordered mutable collections that have values stored under keys.

This page is intentionally left blank

Chapter **4**

Functions and Modular Programming

This chapter covers the basics of working with pre-existing functions and writing our own functions. Functions are blocks of reusable code that perform specific tasks, which allows for better organization and improves reusability. We will also explore how to import libraries that come bundled with Python as well as from other programmers. Finally, we will explore modules and packages.

The key learning objectives of this chapter are:

- Importing functions from Python libraries
- Utilizing PIP to install third-party libraries
- Writing our own functions
- Understanding functions and variable scope
- Working with modules and packages

4.1 Importing Functions from Python Libraries

4.4.1 Introduction to Functions and Modular Programming

At this point, using *functions* should be second nature. We have been using lots of functions like print(), input(), list(), len(), and many more, but we haven't really been thinking about what they really are. We have no idea exactly how print(), for example, does its job. We only know that when we pass an argument, Python somehow prints it to the console. Much like how we don't need to know how an engine works to start up a car, we don't need to know the details of how the print() function works to use it to print out some information. We call this process of hiding complex information *abstraction*, and it's one of the reasons functions are used. Another reason we use functions is to *encapsulate* a set of instructions that we can reuse throughout our code.

Consider the following pseudocode:

```
walk 5 steps forward
turn left
walk 8 steps forward
```

In this case "walk" and "turn" could be considered functions. We wouldn't want to include all of the details of how to walk or how to turn in our pseudocode, but if we did it might look something like this.

```
for steps = 1 to 5:
    move right foot forward
    move left foot forward
endfor
set direction to direction minus 90°
for steps = 1 to 8:
    move right foot forward
    move left foot forward
endfor
```

There are two issues here. First, while it is important that we understand what it means to walk a set number of steps, having that detail here is just distracting, making it harder to understand the point of the instructions. The turning instructions, while accurate, also seem confusing due to their specificity. The other issue is that we are repeating ourselves a fair bit by explaining how to step each time. In essence what we want to do is take that level of detail, write it in detail, hide it away, and reference it whenever we need to.

Breaking our programs into smaller, more manageable pieces, is known as *modular programming*. Modular programming offers many benefits which can be seen in our walking example.

- **Reusability:** Functions can be reused across a program or many programs. Defining how to walk once and then simply referring to it later saves time.

- **Maintainability:** Functions can be changed if needed without modifying the rest of the code. In our walking example, if we needed to use a cane or a walker for mobility issues, we would only need to update our walking function. Otherwise, we would have to rewrite every piece of code that requires walking.

- **Readability:** It is easier to read code that contains functions with a descriptive name than to write out the details each time. If we actually gave instructions to get to a new location by describing it step by step and turn by turn, no one would actually read it.

In addition to these benefits, modular programming also allows for better collaboration. Each team member can focus on a function at a time and bring them back into the main program. This ensures programmers don't get overwhelmed by the complexity of an entire program and also that they don't waste time working on the same task as someone else.

4.1.2 Built-in Libraries

Python *libraries*, also known as modules, are collections of codes that provide additional functionalities to Python. Some of these libraries are built-in to Python, while others need to be installed separately. Some commonly used built-in libraries include:

- **math:** provides extra mathematical functions and constants

- **random:** provides functions for creating random numbers and randomizing events

- **datetime:** provides functions for working with dates, times, and time intervals

- **os:** provides functions for interacting with the operation system, most often files and directories

The functions in these libraries are not available without importing them first. This allows Python to start with just the core functions faster and with less memory use. This also allows for a more customizable experience for programmers. There are so many different reasons to program in Python and some of them rely more heavily on some libraries than others.

There are two ways to import libraries. We can import the entire library, or we can just import the functions we want to use. To import the entire library, the `import` keyword is used followed by the library name. When importing this way the functions are called in reference to the library.

For example, if we wanted to create a program that used square roots to determine the length of a 25 in² square, we could use the following code.

Commands

```
import math
print(math.sqrt(25))
```

Output

```
5
```

`sqrt` is a function inside the math library. Without writing `import math` before using `math.sqrt(25)` we would encounter an *error*. This is however a bit of a waste since we are loading in the entire math library including the trigonometric functions `sin()`, `cos()`, and `tan()`, rounding functions like `ceil()` and `floor()`, and conversion functions like `radians()` and `degrees()`.

To load a specific function we start with which functions we want to import and then which library they belong to. Recreating the square root example:

Commands

```
import sqrt from math
print(sqrt(25))
```

Output

```
5
```

Note that we write `sqrt(25)` instead of `math.sqrt(25)` because we only specifically imported the `sqrt()` function. Our program has no specific information loaded about the math library, and if we tried to use `math.sqrt(25)` in this case, we would receive an error.

Two important notes to make before moving on. First, while you can import libraries and functions on any line before you call them, it is a good practice to import all information at the top of your Python script. Not only is this a good organizational tip, but it also helps others reading your code understand which libraries you will be using. Second, some libraries and functions are commonly abbreviated on import. This is done using the "as" keyword. While you can use this to shorten or modify any library's name, it may cause confusion to others reading your code. So while this is possible, it is not advisable.

Commands

```
import math as jimmy
print(jimmy.sqrt(25))
```

Output

```
5
```

If we wanted to import multiple functions from a library, we can use a comma to separate them in the import statement. We might want to use both the `randint()` and `choice()` functions from the random library. `randint()` choses a random *integer* between two given values while `choice()` picks a random value from a *list*.

Commands

```
from random import randint, choice
random_number = randint(2, 10)
fruits = ['apples', 'bananas', 'cherries']
random_fruit = choice(fruits)
print('I would like', random_number, random_fruit)
```

Output

```
I would like 3 cherries
```

This example picks a random integer between 2 and 10, and a random fruit from the list. This would give several randomized responses such as "I would like 4 bananas" or "I would like 2 cherries".

We can also import everything from a library by using the "*" *wildcard character*. Table 4.1 shows the difference between the two methods of importing everything from a library.

Table 4.1	Importing everything from a library

	Import Random	**From Random Import ***
Getting a random integer	`random.randint(1,10)`	`randint(1,10)`
Getting a random list item	`random.choice(['apples', 'bananas', 'cherries'])`	`choice(['apples', 'bananas', 'cherries'])`

Importing entire libraries should be done sparingly as it increases the overall memory use. It is much more efficient to just import the functions and values that are necessary for the program you are writing.

4.1.3 Third-party Libraries

In addition to the standard libraries, there are many libraries made by other developers. When writing code using a computer-based IDE, these libraries need to be installed using pip, the package installer for Python. The easiest way to do this is in the command prompt of the computer by typing "pip install" followed by the name of the library. When using an online IDE there can be limitations on the number of third-party libraries you can use, but the ones described in this book are commonly used and should be supported by all online IDEs. In REPLIT, for example, when you try to import a library, it will be installed by default, although it may take a minute.

Some common third party libraries include:

- **NumPy:** provides functions for complex mathematical computations and working with arrays

- **Pandas:** provides functions for working with data sets

- **Matplotlib:** provides functions for data visualizations and plots

- **Requests:** provides functions for sending HTTP requests and working with web APIs

- **Beautiful Soup:** provides functions for web scraping

If we wanted to use matplotlib to create a plot of some data, we would first need to install it by typing "pip install matplotlib" in the command prompt. Again, online IDEs should allow you to ignore this step. If a library is installed once, it does not need to be installed again.

Typically, most users of matplotlib are only interested in the pyplot sub-library, or module, of matplotlib, so we can just import that. Since `matplotlib.pyplot.function_name()` is going to be problematic to type multiple times, most programmers abbreviate it to `plt`. There are multiple functions that we would likely use, so we would import the whole library.

In this example, we plot out the temperatures over a week, in Celsius. This is provided as an example of how to use a third-party library, and the details are not important at this point.

```python
import matplotlib.pyplot as plt
# days is a list that will go on the x-axis
#temperatures is a list that will go on the y-axis

days = ['Mon', 'Tue', 'Wed', 'Thu', 'Fri', 'Sat', 'Sun']
temperatures = [18, 20, 22, 21, 19, 23, 24]


# Plotting the data

plt.plot(days, temperatures) #pass in x and y values
plt.xlabel('Day of the Week') #set x-axis label
plt.ylabel('Temperature (°C)') #set y-axis label
#set the title of the plot
plt.title('Average Daily Temperature over a Week')
plt.show() # Display the plot
```

Figure 4.1   **Changes in temperature over a week, created by the preceding code**

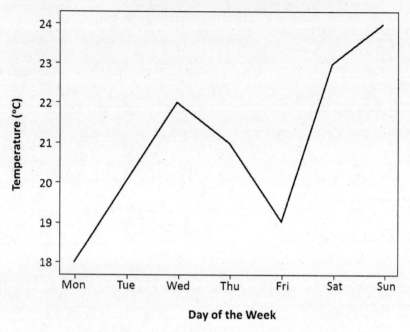

While you might not know all of the functions in the pyplot library, the code is very readable and easy to follow. We can also see how abstraction is useful here. We do not need to know how plt.plot() creates a graph or how plt.title() sets the title, but we can know how to use them to create a graph.

Matplotlib gives us the ability to visualize data in a straightforward way without needing to worry about the dealing of creating and rendering graphics in Python. This lets us focus on analyzing results without getting bogged down in the details. This is abstraction at its finest.

By using well-established libraries, we can leverage the time and effort put in by programmers who have come before us.

While we can write our own code to handle large sets of data, it makes more sense to use code from the Numpy library, for example, which has been developed, tested, and optimized for performance. We will explore a variety of libraries, each with their own applications, as we continue on our programming journey.

4.2 Writing Your Own Functions

Writing our own functions will allow us to create reusable blocks of code to perform different common tasks. We can encapsulate common operations to make our code more organized and easier to maintain.

A function in Python uses the `def` keyword followed by the name of the function and a pair of parentheses. The parentheses will contain any *parameters* required for the function to perform its task. The body of the code is indented, just like when we use *for-loops* or `if` statements. We may also want to return some information from our function by using an optional `return` keyword.

An important step missed by many novice programmers is including a *docstring*, which is a description of the function including any parameters and values that are returned. Docstrings are not required, but improve readability and make it easier for other programmers to reuse our code. Docstrings are surrounded by three quotation marks and may take up multiple lines if necessary.

The basic structure of a function is:

```
def function_name(parameters):
    """Docstring instructions"""
    function body
    return value
```

For our first custom function, we can address a mathematical topic dreaded by junior high students: surface area! Any surface area formula makes a great function. We have a number of values to pass in and a value to return. The calculation is complex enough that we may want to move it away from the main part of our code, but simple enough that we should understand coding it. Functions should only have a single job, so it is best to write a function for each shape. We will use the surface area of a cylinder.

The approach here is to take in the height and radius of the cylinder and use the formula for the surface area of a cylinder, SA = 2 * π * radius * (radius + height). Some people are more familiar with the formula in the form SA = 2 * π *radius * height + 2 π r2, but either will give the same results. Since we are using π, we should import it from the math library. We could also estimate this to 3.14 if we were less concerned with accuracy. Since the surface area of cylinders tends to produce values with lots of decimal values, we will also pass in an optional parameter for how much we want to round our result.

Commands

```
from math import pi

def calculate_cylinder_surface_area(radius, height,
places = 1):
    """
    Calculate the surface area of a cylinder.
    The surface area of a cylinder is given by the formula:
    2 * π * radius * (radius + height)

    Parameters:
    radius (float): The radius of the base of the cylinder.
    height (float): The height of the cylinder.

    Returns:
    float: The surface area of the cylinder.

    Example:
    >>> calculate_cylinder_surface_area(3, 5)
    150.8
    """
    surface_area = 2 * pi * radius * (radius + height)
    surface_area = round(surface_area,places)
    return surface_area

sa = calculate_cylinder_surface_area(2,4))
print(sa)
```

Output

```
75.4.
```

Let's look at this in more detail:

`from math import pi`	We also need the value of pi from the math library, so we use the "from ... import ..." format

`def calculate_cylinder_`
`surface_area(radius,`
`height, places = 1):`
	Here is the function definition. Note that we are taking in the radius and height, in that order. places is an optional parameter and is set to 1 if it is not supplied on function call.

`"""`
`Calculate the surface`
`area of a cylinder.`
`The surface area of a`
`cylinder is given by`
`the formula:`
`2 * π * radius * (radius`
`+ height)`
 	
`Parameters:`
`radius (float): The`
`radius of the base of`
`the cylinder.`
`height (float): The`
`height of the cylinder.`
 	
`Returns:`
`float: The surface area`
`of the cylinder.`
 	
`Example:`
`>>>`
`calculate_cylinder_`
`surface_area(3, 5)`
`150.8`
`"""`
	Most of this function is actually the docstring. Normally you wouldn't go into this much detail with such a simple function. However we can see several key pieces of information common to docstrings.
	• Description of the function
	• Parameters along with the expected data type, name, and description
	• Return value and the type
	• An example of how to use it
	
	At the bare minimum we should provide a description.

`surface_area = 2 * pi`
`* radius * (radius +`
`height)`
`surface_area =`
`round(surface_`
`area,places)`
	Finally, the actual code. Here the surface area is mathematically calculated and rounded.

`return surface_area`	This returns the value stored in surface_area to the function call. We don't need a return, but without it the value of surface_area is not available to the rest of the program.

`sa = calculate_cylinder_`
`surface_area(2,4))`
`print(sa)`
	This is the function call from the main body of the program. The returned value is stored in sa and printed to the console.

Custom functions do not run without being called, so it is important to include a function call within the main body of our code, or nothing will happen. It is also possible to call functions within other functions and even to call a function within itself, a technique called recursion.

There are several important things to consider when writing your own functions. Like with *variables,* be sure to use descriptive names. Functions are typically named after the action they perform. Include docstrings to document your function. This is useful for those who may want to reuse our code, or to us when we revisit old code that we have written before. We also have to ensure that our functions only perform one task. This makes it easier to properly test them to ensure there are no issues with them.

4.3 Understanding Functions and Variable Scope

Before we continue, a quick note about terminology. We have been using the phrase "parameters" when describing the values passed into the function, but back when we were calling functions we called them "arguments". This can cause some confusion but mixing up these terms won't hurt our programs, just our ability to talk about them. In technical terms, parameters are the values that the function receives and are used by the function. Arguments are the values we pass into the function when we call it from another part of the code.

This doesn't answer the question as to why we need to pass in the information at all. If we have the information within the program, why do we need to tell the function what its information is? Shouldn't it already know? The answer is not as simple as it may seem.

Variables have a scope, that is to say that they can only be accessed by certain parts of the code. Variables that are defined within the main body of our code have global scope, meaning that they can be read by all parts of the code, including inside of our functions. The variables within our functions have local scope, meaning that they are only available within our function while it is running. This is why we need to return values to the main body. If we didn't, the calculated information would be lost.

Ideally, we don't use *global variables* within our functions to make them more reusable, but there are times when it is simply convenient to use them. To avoid confusion, it is also recommended that we use different variable names within our functions compared to the main body of the code, but this is not always worth worrying about. The scope of variables will take care of this issue, but it can lead to some issues with readability.

For example:

```
def my_function():
    x = 10
    print("The local value of x is",x)

x = 20
my_function()
print("The global value of x is", x)
```

Here we get the messages "The local value of x is 10" and "The global value of x is 20" printed to the console. We set the value of x to 20, so globally it is 20. Inside the function we set the local value of x to 10, so inside the function x is 10. This should help us see why avoiding the same variable name for local and global variables is a good idea, but this is mainly for readability.

A similar example:

```
Commands
def my_function():
    print("The value of y inside the function is", y)

y = 20
my_function()
print("The value of y outside the function is",y)
```

```
Output
The value of y inside the function is 20
The value of y outside the function is 20
```

Since y is not defined inside the function, we default to the global value, so the value is reported as 20 both times.

We can change a local variable in a function to a global variable by using the global keyword.

Commands

```
def my_function():
    global z
    z += 10
    print("The value of z inside the function is", z)

z= 20
my_function()
print("The value of z outside the function is",z)
```

Output

```
The value of z inside the function is 30
The value of z outside the function is 30
```

This tells the function that it should reference the global variable z. Any changes to z in the function are made to the global version of z. This is not good practice, but there may be situations where there are no simple alternatives. The better alternative is to pass in the global value, modify the local copy, return the value, and restore it in the same variable name.

Commands

```
def my_function(z):
    #this is the local copy of z
    z += 10
    print("The value of z inside the function is", z)
    return z

#this is the global z
z= 20
z = my_function(z)
print("The value of z outside the function is",z)
```

Output

```
The value of z inside the function is 30
The value of z outside the function is 30
```

Again, it would be better to use a different variable name in this case so that we understand whether we are looking at a local variable or a global variable, but this is still a better case.

Let's look at a more practical example to help better understand scope. If we were creating software for a retail outlet it would be very helpful to have a function that could apply a discount to a price. We would also want to be able to reuse this function in many programs as it is quite a common operation.

Figure 4.2   Example of a weekend sale at a retail outlet

Photo by Markus Spiske, published November 1, 2019, Unsplash, https://unsplash.com/photos/weekend-sale-signage-5UJbKYUjFCk

While the price of the item and the discount rate would likely be saved as global variables, we can't be sure that they would have the same variable names in each sales program that we create, so it is better to use parameters when we create the function and to pass in the global variables from the program.

Commands

```
def discounted_price(original_price, discount_rate):
    """
    Takes an original_price (float) and a discount_rate,
    as a decimal (float).
    Returns the price (float), rounded to 2 decimal
    places
    """
    price = original_price * (1-discount_rate)
    price = round(price,2)
    return price
sweater_cost = 54.99
percent_off = 0.40
discounted_sweater = discounted_price(sweater_cost,
                        percent_off)
print("The sweater now costs $", discounted_sweater)
```

Output

```
The sweater now costs $ 32.99
```

The scope of original_price, discount_rate, and price are all local. The scope of sweater_cost, percent_off, and discounted_sweater are all global. While we could have used our global values of sweater_cost and percent_off inside of our function, then it would require modification if we wanted to reuse the function for a pizza place, for example. We could really copy and paste this code into any number of retail programs. To improve reusability, our functions should be as general as possible. Note as well that to avoid confusion, we used very specific variables for our global variables.

Functions should be designed as separate pieces of code that have no idea what is happening in the rest of our program, other than what we pass in. We provide the information on a need to know basis through parameters, and ask for a result to be returned to the point in the program where the function call was made. While not always 100% possible, this approach will help write more modular, reusable code.

4.4 Working with Modules and Packages

4.4.1 Understanding Modules and Packages

So far we have been writing all of our code in one Python file, but this single file can quickly grow to an unmanageable size as our project complexity grows. Using modules and packages allows us to break down our code into smaller, more manageable pieces and separate them into separate files. This allows us to find problems and update the code quickly. It also allows us to work more efficiently as a team. As we discussed with functions, modules take this teamwork a whole step further. Now team members can work on their own individual files and bring them together to the team.

You can think of modules and packages as fulfilling the same roles as functions, but to a much higher degree. Instead of abstracting away the details to a separate function in another part of our file, we can take these functions and move them into an entirely different function. While functions can be copied out of our code and pasted into another project, we can reuse the entire module in another project.

When working with modules, we want to have a main Python file that serves as our starting point. For many projects, we will simply call this main.py, but we can call it whatever we want. As a side note, if we are using an online IDE, it may require the file to be called main.py, but that is a requirement of the service and not Python itself. The other files will be imported into our main file by using the import statement exactly like we did in section 4.1.

As an example, consider a program written to help people with large movie collections. We would need a `main.py` file to tie everything together, but we may also want to have separate files to handle some of the other pieces. For example, we may want to have a file that contains all the functions related to organizing our collection, such as sorting, adding, and removing items. We could call this `collection.py`. This file could be reused for other types of collections as well, making it very reusable. We may want a file to handle the specifics of collecting the information associated with a movie. This could contain functions for recording titles, giving reviews, and setting genres. We could call this `movie.py`. While these functions would be fairly specific and the module might not be reusable, hiding these details would make it easier to read our main file.

It wouldn't be hard for us to imagine other files that could handle other specific parts of our program. Perhaps `user.py` could handle the user interaction. Maybe `interface.py` could handle the graphical user inference. The important thing is to break the larger program into smaller, self-contained, pieces.

While we won't go into it in detail, packages just take this slightly further. If we felt that our movie modules could be reusable as a complete piece, then we could organize them as a package. Instead of a `main.py` file to hold them all together, we put all the files in our package into a folder with a special file called `__init__.py`. This file doesn't technically have to contain any information, but it is required so that Python understands that it is looking at a package and not just a directory with a bunch of unrelated Python files. We looked at matplotlib earlier in the chapter, which is an example of a package.

4.4.2 Creating Modules

Earlier we wrote a function which calculated the surface area of a cylinder. We can expand this example to better illustrate how modules work. Here the approach will be to have each shape represented in its own Python file and then have a `main.py` file which knits them together. We will only write the `cylinder.py` in full for illustrative purposes, but the other modules would have similar functions. To save space, we will write simplified docstrings, but for a proper module we should be including all of the details.

```python
# cylinder.py
import math

def calculate_surface_area(radius, height,places=1):
    """
    Calculate the surface area of a cylinder.
    """
    sa = 2 * math.pi * radius * (radius + height)
    return round(sa, places)

def calculate_volume(radius, height, places = 1):
    """
    Calculate the volume of a cylinder.
    """
    return round(math.pi * radius**2 * height, places)
```

It shouldn't be too hard to imagine what `rectangular_prism.py` or `pyramind.py` would also look like. By keeping these functions in their own files, we can work on them independent of the main program and keep the main file shorter and more readable. Next, we will look at how we would use these modules.

In our main.py, we will need to import these modules, since we will likely have a calculate_surface_area() and a calculate_volume() function in each module, we have to be careful how we import these. There are two main ways to handle this. First, we can just import the entire module and reference the functions with a dot notation.

Commands

```
import rectangular_prism.py
import cylinder.py
import pyramid.py

#find surface area of a 3 x 4 x 8 rectangular prism
sa = rectangular_prism.calculate_surface_area(3,4,8)
print("For a 3x4x8 rectangular prism")
print("The surface area is",sa, "cm squared" )

#find the volume of a cylinder with radius 2.5
#and a height of 5
volume = cylinder.calculate_volume(2.5,5)
print("A cylinder with a radius of 2.5 and height of 5")
print("Has a volume of", volume, "cm cubed")
```

Output

```
For a 3x4x8 rectangular prism
The surface area is 136 cm squared
A cylinder with a radius of 2.5 and height of 5
Has a volume of 98.2 cm cubed
```

As you can imagine, this method, although useful, can be clumsy to work with. Instead we can use the "import from" method and use the "as" keyword to rename the reused functions.

Commands

```
from rectangular_prism import (
    calculate_surface_area as rp_sa,
    calculate_volume as rp_volume
)
from cylinder import (
    calculate_surface_area as cyl_sa,
    calculate_volume as cyl_volume
)
from pyramid import (
    calculate_surface_area as pyramid_sa,
    calculate_volume as pyramid_volume
)
#find surface area of a 3 x 4 x 8 rectangular prism
sa = rp_sa(3,4,8)
print("For a 3x4x8 rectangular prism")
print("The surface area is",sa, "cm squared")
#find the volume of a cylinder with radius 2.5
#and a height of 5
volume = cyl_volume(2.5,5)
print("A cylinder with a radius of 2.5 and height of 5")
print("Has a volume of", volume, "cm cubed")
```

Output

```
For a 3x4x8 rectangular prism
The surface area is 136 cm squared
A cylinder with a radius of 2.5 and height of 5
Has a volume of 98.2 cm cubed
```

This method requires a little more work upfront, but allows us to avoid overwriting functions with the same name and lets us call the functions in a much simpler context. We could have just given our functions in our modules different names, but we want them to be standalone pieces. When writing them we should not need to consider other parts of the code. We also want to be able to use them in other projects and we can't possibly avoid every possible duplication of function names.

One thing that we may notice when reading other programmers' code, is the use of a special `if` statement: `if __name__=='__main__'`. This special *conditional statement* will only run if a file is run directly, that is to say, that it is the main file we are targeting. This allows us to test and debug a module by giving commands that will only be executed if we run it directly. For example, in our cylinder code, we could write some test code to ensure the surface area and volume functions are returning the correct values.

Commands

```python
import math

def calculate_sa(radius, height, places = 1):
    """
    Calculate the surface area of a cylinder.
    """
    return round(2 * math.pi * radius * (radius +
height), places)

def calculate_vol(radius, height, places = 1):
    """
    Calculate the volume of a cylinder.
    """
    return round(math.pi * radius**2 * height, places)
if __name__ == '__main__':
    print("Cylinder with radius 5 and height 10")
    print("should have a volume of 785 cm cubed")
    print("Result 1 decimal:", calculate_vol(5,10))
    print("Result 2 decimal:", calculate_ vol(5,10,2))
    print("Cylinder with radius 5 and height 10")
    print("should have surface area of 471 cm squared")
    print("Result 1 decimal:", calculate_sa(5,10))
    print("Result 2 decimal:", calculate_sa(5,10,2))
```

Output

```
Cylinder with radius 5 and height 10
should have a volume of 785 cm cubed
Result 1 decimal: 785.4
Result 2 decimal: 785.4
Cylinder with radius 5 and height 10
should have surface area of 471 cm squared
Result 1 decimal: 471.2
Result 2 decimal: 471.24
```

From our results, we see that the functions are returning the correct values, however, there is an issue with rounding in some cases. Unfortunately for us, the round() function removes trailing zeros even if we want them to be included. If this is important then we can work on it within our module without having to worry about the rest of our code which can be a huge time saver! If we were to run our main.py file directly then the cylinder code is no longer the main file and the testing code we wrote will not run. This way we do not have to delete or comment out our module testing code when working with the whole program.

Getting used to writing code in this way will save us time in the long run, but it does take some getting used to it. When programmers first start writing code, it is natural to only use a single file to contain all of the required functions and code. However, with experience we begin to see how modular programming can help with organization, reusability, and collaboration, making it an extremely important approach to programming.

In the next chapter, we will explore object-oriented programming, a powerful technique that may change the way we work with Python. This will allow us to continue writing more modular code that can be easier to read and understand.

Quiz

1. **What is the purpose of functions?**
   a. To create variables
   b. To organize code
   c. To reduce crashes
   d. To speed up code

2. **Which keyword is used to define a function?**
   a. def
   b. define
   c. function
   d. pass

3. **What is the purpose of the `import` keyword?**
   a. It creates a new function
   b. It defines a new variable
   c. It loads external libraries and functions
   d. It prints information to the console

4. **A programmer wants to include the line `math.sqrt(16)` within their code. Which line has to be written before this line?**
   a. import math
   b. from math import sqrt
   c. from sqrt import math
   d. import sqrt

5. **Which statement imports the `randint()` function from the "random" library, without the rest of the library?**

   a. from random import randint

   b. from randint import random

   c. import randint

   d. import random

6. **What is the advantage of importing specific functions rather than an entire library?**

   a. it ensures there are no errors

   b. it makes code more modular

   c. it reduces memory uses

   d. it reduces the need of using "pip"

7. **What is the purpose of the "as" keyword in an import statement?**

   a. To import a library

   b. To rename a library or function

   c. To shorten the import statement

   d. To specify the library version

8. **What is the purpose of "pip"?**

   a. To import libraries

   b. To install third-party libraries

   c. To document libraries

   d. To write custom modules

9. **Which library is included with Python and does not need to be installed?**

   a. Pandas

   b. Math

   c. Matplotlib

   d. NumPy

10. **A variable, "scope", is defined inside of a function. Which statement is true?**

    a. "scope" can be accessed anywhere in the program

    b. "scope" can only be accessed inside the function

    c. Variables cannot be defined inside functions

    d. Variables can only be passed into functions as arguments

Answers	1 – b	2 – a	3 – c	4 – a	5 – a
	6 – c	7 – b	8 – b	9 – b	10 – b

Chapter Summary

◆ Functions are reusable blocks of code that perform specific tasks.

◆ Understanding variable scope is important for avoiding crashes and bugs in code.

◆ Importing functions extends the capabilities of Python and allows us to write more complex code without worrying about the details.

◆ Custom functions can improve overall code readability and maintainability.

◆ Modular programming improves the organization, reusability, abstraction, and scalability of code.

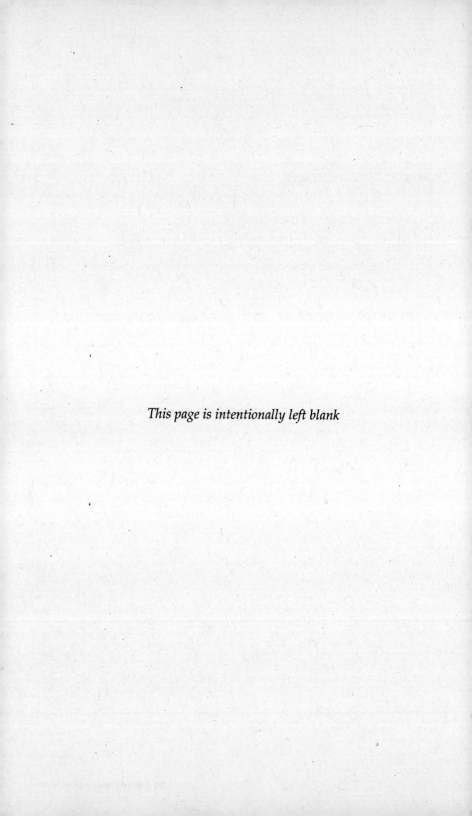

This page is intentionally left blank

Chapter 5

Object-Oriented Programming

In this chapter, we will approach a game-changing, but challenging topic: object-oriented programming. We will investigate what an object is in Python and how we use classes to create instances of the class. It is easy to get bogged down in the terminology, but if we master the concept, object-oriented programming can allow us to write clean, modular code in a way that functions and modules never would allow.

The key learning objectives of this chapter are:

- Understanding the core concepts of object-oriented programming

- Creating and using classes and objects

- Applying inheritance and composition to our classes

- Understanding how to encapsulate data and control access from outside classes

5.1 Understanding Object-Oriented Concepts

So far, we have been programming in a manner which can be referred to as *procedural programming*. This method of programming focuses on writing statements and functions that operate on *variables* in a very sequential manner. Python also has the ability to allow for *object-oriented programming*. This approach focuses on objects as the backbone of programming. *Objects* are self-contained entities that combine data and functions, typically known as *methods*. Earlier when we looked at *data structures*, we noted that they allow us to simplify some of the tasks that would be complicated to complete without them. Objects act in the same manner, allowing us to simplify tasks that would be more complicated to manage without them.

Figure 5.1	Image of a book

Photo by Kenny Eliason, published on February 1, 2017, Unsplash, https://unsplash.com/photos/black-case-3MGbXrdV8Mo

If we think of a book as an object, then it would have attributes such as the author, the publisher, the genre, and many other characteristics. Additionally, there are actions we might associate with the book. For example, we could define methods for looking up information in the table of contents to find the correct section, checking definitions in a glossary, or simply navigating from page to page.

If we were to write a program that would store all of this information using our current method, we would need to store all of the information within individual variables. Instead we can use an object to store this information. Of course, we could have also used a *dictionary* to store the raw data, but it lacks the ability to store the methods associated with the book.

With reusability in mind, we construct the book as a class, essentially a template for creating a book, which can be reused to create many book objects with their own characteristics. This will eliminate the need for so many variables to keep track of all attributes of the books.

This gives us a powerful new framework for approaching programming which allows us to make much more streamlined, reusable code. Objects also lend themselves to the concepts of encapsulation and abstraction discussed in the previous chapter, giving us the opportunity to further distance the fine details from the specifics of our code. A common example used is that while a car needs to have many processes that interact with each other, the drivers don't need to concern themselves with the particular details. We don't need to understand how the car takes the gasoline from the fuel tank and provides it to the engine to finally produce the motion that we desire, we really just need to know that we keep the tank full and press the gas pedal. Abstracting away the details leads to a cleaner code.

Table 5.1 shows some of the differences between procedural programming and object-oriented programming (OOP).

Table 5.1	Procedural Programming vs Object-Oriented Programming
Procedural Programming	**Object-Oriented Programming**
Code is organized into functions	Code is organized into classes
Functions promote reusability	Techniques such as inheritance and polymorphism enhance reusability
Data and functions are separate	Data and functions are bundled together
Suitable for small to medium-sized programs	Better for larger, more complex systems

Many programs utilize a mixture of procedural and object-oriented programming. As beginners, we may not need to fully utilize OOP, but we need to understand that it exists, and utilize it where appropriate for our programs.

5.2 Classes and Objects in Python

Now that we understand the concept of objects, it's important to understand how classes and objects are used in Python. We use classes in Python as a template for creating objects. You can think of these as blueprints. Classes define attributes and methods that respectively represent the data that the object will contain and the functions that it has. Before creating a class, we should consider the attributes that the objects will need to have. A book class could include information about a title, author, and publisher.

Creating classes is similar to functions, but differs in a few key areas. Classes start with the new word "class" and class names are capitalized by convention to make them visually different from functions and variables. In cases where two or more words are used to name a class, we should use capitalized letters for each word, often stylized as CapWords.[10] While there are times you will need to add parenthesis, they are optional for now, so again by convention, we will not include them.

```
class Book:
    def __init__(self, title, author, publisher):
        self.title = title
        self.author = author
        self.publisher = publisher
```

Here you can see that we set up a new class, called Book. In a block under the class is something that looks an awful lot like a function, but since it is part of a class, we refer to it as a method. Like a typical function it has *parameters* and an indented block of code, but things get a little weirder from there.

First, you might notice the double underscores surrounding "init". This serves two purposes. First, it shows that __init__ is a special method with a specific role in Python programming. Second, it avoids any naming conflicts if a programmer wants to create a variable named "init". __init__ is known as a constructor and is called whenever we create a new copy of our class, called an instance. The constructor is often used to set the attributes of the instance that makes it unique.

To create new instances of our book class, we write the name of the class followed by the *arguments* in rounded brackets. Here

---

10. PEP 8, "PEP 8 -Style Guide for Python Code," Python.org, accessed August 1, 2024, https://peps.python.org/pep-0008/.

we are creating objects representing "Pride and Prejudice" and "Moby Dick".

```
book1 = Book("Pride and Prejudice","Jane Austen",
        "T.Egerton, Whitehall")
book2 = Book("Moby Dick", "Herman Melville",
        "Harper & Brothers")
```

Commands
```
print("Book 1 Details:")
print("Title:", book1.title)
print("Author:", book1.author)
print("Publisher:", book1.publisher)

print("\nBook 2 Details:")
print("Title:", book2.title)
print("Author:", book2.author)
print("Publisher:", book2.publisher)
```

Output
```
Book 1 Details:
Title: Pride and Prejudice
Author: Jane Austen
Publisher: T. Egerton, Whitehall

Book 2 Details:
Title: Moby Dick
Author: Herman Melville
Publisher: Harper & Brothers
```

This direct method of access is great when we want to initially start working with classes since it is convenient, but keep in mind that we typically want to encapsulate our classes like we did with our functions. To put it another way, we want to handle all of the data about the object within the class. Our objects should be able to stand on their own outside of the main body of code.

We can also see that this would not be maintainable if we wanted to print out information on an entire bookshelf. With only two books, we are repeating ourselves, something we want to avoid when writing code. Instead we can write a method to print a summary of the book's details.

Commands

```
class Book:
    def __init__(self, title, author, publisher):
        self.title = title
        self.author = author
        self.publisher = publisher

    def display_details(self):
        print("Title:", self.title)
        print("Author:", self.author)
        print("Publisher:", self.publisher)
        print()

book1 = Book("Pride and Prejudice","Jane Austen",
        "T. Egerton, Whitehall")
book2 = Book("Moby Dick", "Herman Melville",
        "Harper & Brothers")

book1.display_details()
book2.display_details()
```

Output

```
Title: Pride and Prejudice
Author: Jane Austen
Publisher: T. Egerton, Whitehall

Title: Moby Dick
Author: Herman Melville
Publisher: Harper & Brothers
```

When creating instance methods, the keyword `self` must be the first parameter to refer to the instance, the particular version, of the object we are working with. Again, the same as creating the instance, we do not actually pass it in. Python handles that part for us. A big pitfall for new programmers is to forget to write `self.title` or `self.author`. If we were to only write title we would get an error since there is no variable defined as title, there is only the instance attribute `self.title`.

5.3 Inheritance and Composition

5.3.1 Inheritance

Inheritance is a fundamental concept in object-oriented programming. Inheritance allows one class to inherit attributes and methods from another class, much like children inherit traits from their parents. With this in mind, it's not surprising that the class whose properties and methods are inherited is referred to as the *parent class*, or sometimes the *superclass*, and the class who inherits the properties and methods is the *child class*, or *subclass*. Parent classes tend to be more general, with child classes being more specific. This pattern of inheritance allows for the creation of complex yet reusable code.

Figure 5.2	Chess pieces on chess board

Photo by Rafael Rex Felisilda, published January 20, 2021, Unsplash, https://unsplash.com/photos/chess-pieces-on-chess-board-U_Kz2RnfFAk

If we think about a chess set, it contains many pieces. These pieces are similar in many ways but have many attributes that make them different as well. Table 5.2 shows some of the properties and methods that could be used to create classes for each chess piece. We won't wonder about the specifics of playing chess, but we should be able to see that the pieces are similar in some ways and different in others.

Table 5.2 **Properties and methods associated with chess pieces**

	Pawn	Knight	Bishop	Rook	Queen	King
Properties	color position captured moved blocked	color position captured	color position captured	color position captured moved	color position captured	color position captured moved check
Methods	move() promote() capture_ move()	move()	move()	move() castle()	move()	move() in_ check() castle()

From this table, we can see that writing the code for each class is going to lead to some repetition which is something we want to avoid. To combat this, we can use a parent class to hold all the similar properties and methods, which we could call ChessPiece.

We can think of a class ChessPiece as being a parent class and the particular pieces as being child classes. Our ChessPiece would be defined to set the color and position of the piece as defined by the creation of the instance, with the captured property set to False by default. Since the .move() method for each piece would be different, there is no real sense of defining it in our parent class.

```
class ChessPiece:
    def __init__(self, color, position):
        self.color = color
        self.position = position
        self.captured = False
```

To create a child class, we use the same format as all of our other classes except we put the name of the parent class in round brackets after the class name. So, for a Pawn class, we might write:

```
class Pawn(ChessPiece):
    def __init__(self, color, position):
        super().__init__(color, position):
            self.moved = False
            self.blocked = False
```

Since the color, position, and if it is captured are handled in the parent class, we do not need to rewrite that code in the child class. Instead we write super().__init__(color, position) within our constructor to run that piece of code within the parent. Using super() lets us refer back to the parent when necessary.

The remainder of our Pawn class could look like this:

```
def move(self, new_position):
    self.position = new_position
    self.moved = True

def promote(self):
    self.status = "Queen"

def capture_move(self):
    return "Pawn captures another piece"
```

This lets us build on our ChessPiece class, reusing the pieces that apply to the Pawn class. We could apply this concept to all of the other pieces such as knights and queens.

5.3.2 Composition

When we use inheritance, we are stating that the new class, such as a Pawn, is a version of the old class, such as a ChessPiece. This pattern reoccurs throughout programming. A child Cat class is a version of a parent Animal class. A Button could be the child of an Input class. Composition has a slightly different relationship. Composition is used when an object contains another object. If we think about a car, it is actually made up of many objects. From a programming point of view, we could make classes for each object that makes up a car elsewhere in our code, and then add those in as properties of the car class. This is much easier to see with an example. We could make a simplified version of an Engine class and a Wheels class.

```python
class Engine:
    def start(self):
        return "Engine started"

class Wheels:
    def roll(self):
        return "Wheels rolling"
```

Once our base Engine and Wheels classes are created, we can use them within our Car class. We do this by assigning instances of them as attributes. We can then use the methods and attribute associated with these classes within our Car class.

```python
class Car:
    def __init__(self):
        self.engine = Engine()
        self.wheels = Wheels()

    def start(self):
        return self.engine.start()

    def move(self):
        return self.wheels.roll()
```

Composition is an extremely useful technique for making fairly complex classes without a lot of visible complexity. By abstracting away the details with the base class, we can write code that is easier to update and understand.

5.4 Polymorphism and Method Overriding

Polymorphism is an important concept in object-oriented programming and builds on our work on inheritance, but now we will focus on *method overriding*. In Python, all classes that we create are subclasses of the built-in "object" class and therefore have inherited all of the methods and attributes associated with it. We have already been overriding some of these methods without even knowing it. For example, the object class has a built-in __init__ method which we have been overriding to create our own constructors. This is why we could still create classes without __init__ if we didn't need any default values to be passed in. Every class by default uses the object class __init__ method, unless we override it.

A slightly less abstract example is the object class __str__ method. This method determines the behavior of the object when we use the print() function on it. By default, we get an output which includes the class name and the memory address of the instance, but that is not very useful to us as programmers. We can modify this behavior by overriding the method as shown below.

Default __str__ vs Overriding __str__

Default Behavior

Commands

```
class Dog:
    def __init__(self,name,sound):
        self.name = name
        self.sound = sound
    def speak(self):
        print(self.name, "says", self.sound)

dog = Dog("Daisy", "woof")
dog.speak()
print(dog)
```

Output

```
Daisy says woof
<__main__.Dog object at 0x0000020E5C9CBC40>
```

Custom behavior

Commands

```
class Dog:
    def __init__(self,name,sound):
        self.name = name
        self.sound = sound
    def speak(self):
        print(self.name, "says", self.sound)
    def __str__(self):
        return "This is an instance of the Dog class"

dog = Dog("Daisy", "woof")
dog.speak()
print(dog)
```

Output

```
Daisy says woof
This is an instance of the Dog class
```

Since we need to return a single string from our __str__ method, we should take a moment to discuss formatted strings, more commonly known as *f-strings*. F-strings allow us to write strings that include the variable values, eliminating the need for all the commas we have been using with our print statements. For example, one of our first examples in this book was printing a hello statement. Table 5.3 shows three ways we could have accomplished this.

Table 5.3	**Printing with variables**	
Comma separated arguments	`name = "Jimmy"` `print("Hello", name)`	Only works within print function

Concatenated strings	`name = "Jimmy"`
	 `print("Hello " +`
	 `name)`
		Only works with strings

F-strings	`name = "Jimmy"`
	 `print(f"Hello`
	 `{name}")`
		Starts with "f". Variables wrapped with curly brackets and inside quotations.

F-strings are a natural way to improve our class to make the code cleaner and to make our output more informative.

```
Commands
class Dog:
    def __init__(self,name,sound):
        self.name = name
        self.sound = sound
    def speak(self):
        print(f"{self.name} says {self.sound}")
    def __str__(self):
        return f"{self.name} is an instance of Dog"
dog = Dog("Daisy", "woof")
dog.speak()
print(dog)

Output
Daisy says woof
Daisy is an instance of the Dog class
```

F-strings can even contain functions and simple arithmetic within them, making them a much more compact and versatile way of writing strings. Moving forward in the book we will focus on f-strings for writing strings.

There are many built-in methods in the object class that are inherited by any custom class that we create, which we may encounter on our programming journey. This includes methods for determining how to compare instances of the class and how to handle truth values, among other things, but this is beyond the scope of this book.[11]

Typically, we like to use polymorphism with inheritance to create more detailed subclasses. In our examples in Chapter 4, we didn't need to override any methods, but this is typically not the case. For example, if we were writing a program for a business, they might want an "Employee" class with attributes and methods that would be relevant to all employees. They may also want an "Intern" class which is similar, but not identical to "Employee". Polymorphism and method overriding will come in handy here. Our "Employee" class can be seen in the following code:

A simplified "Employee" class

```python
class Employee:
    def __init__(self, name, salary, pay_periods):
        self.name = name
        self.salary = salary
        self.pay_periods = pay_periods
    def calculate_pay(self):
        return round(self.salary/self.pay_periods,2)
    def calculate_bonus(self):
        bonus = self.salary * 0.10
        print(self.name, "receives a bonus of", bonus)
```

11. Python Documentation, "3. Data model – Python 3.12.4 documentation" accessed June 16, 2024 https://docs.python.org/3/reference/datamodel.html

Our "Intern" class would be very similar. We would still want to store the intern's name, salary, and number of pay periods. We also would want to calculate how much they were paid, but it is unlikely that we would pay them a bonus. Since we are duplicating a lot of the Employee class, it makes sense to make it the parent, but we will need to override the .calculate_bonus() method. The following code illustrates our Intern class.

A simplified "Intern" class

```
class Intern(Employee):
    def calculate_bonus(self):
        print(self.name, "is an intern")
        print("No bonus")
```

Since "Intern" is a child class of "Employee" it contains all of the methods in "Employee" so we do not need to redefine them. So "Intern" can still use the .calculate_pay() method and its own version of the .calculate_bonus() method.

Commands
```
manager = Employee("Alice", 80000,26)
developer = Employee("Bob", 60000,26)
intern = Intern("Charlie", 30000,12)
manager.calculate_bonus()
developer.calculate_bonus()
print(f"{developer.name} receives")
print(f"${developer.calculate_pay()} pay")
intern.calculate_bonus()
print(f"{intern.name} receives")
print(f"${intern.calculate_pay()} pay")
```

Output
```
Alice receives a bonus of 8000.0
Bob receives a bonus of 6000.0
Bob receives
$2307.69 pay
Charlie is an intern
No bonus
Charlie receives $2500.0 pay
```

Our child and parent relationships can get quite complex as we continue. Figure 5.3 shows how we might create a "Device" class, which has a child class of "Computer", which could, in turn, have a child class of "Laptop". The "Object" class is the parent of all classes without an explicitly stated parent.

Figure 5.3 **A chain of parent-to-child classes**

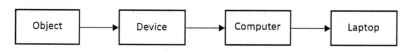

If we had an instance of the "Laptop" class called laptop, and we tried to use a `.boot()` method, Python would first check to see if there is a `.boot()` method inside of the "Laptop" class. If there is then that method runs, regardless if any of the parent classes also has a `.boot()` method. If there is no `.boot()` method in the "Laptop" class, then we check the "Computer" class and continue up the chain until we find a `.boot()` method. If we get back to the "Object" class, which does not have a `.boot()` method, then we get an *AttributeError*.

Understanding polymorphism is an important part of managing complex relationships between custom objects and will be an essential skill on our programming journey.

5.5 Encapsulation

Encapsulation is a technique where we try to write classes that are as separate from the rest of our code as possible. The goal is to write classes that set and modify their own data, return information to the rest of our program, and limit the ability of the rest of the code to change things. Preventing direct access to the values of a class or instance prevents accidental modification of data which could lead to unexpected results or loss of data.

The key tools for encapsulating a class are access modifiers. So far, the attributes of our classes have been public. *Public attributes* are accessible from anywhere in the program and therefore give us less control and security. When working with a team, another member could write code that interacts directly with this information, changing it in ways that we did not anticipate, causing issues with other parts of our class.

If we created, for example, a user account class, we would have rules for changing passwords by making sure the user entered their current password for verification and then we would check if the password is an appropriate length and made up of the correct types of characters. If the password attribute is public, another developer could allow the user to set the value directly without these checks, potentially leading to invalid passwords being used.

Besides public, there are also protected and *private attributes*. Protected attributes indicate to programmers that they should not be accessing and modifying these values directly. Python doesn't explicitly prevent them from doing so, but the naming convention does let them know that they should be so at their own risk. It's a bit like labeling your lunch in the office fridge. Another co-worker could access your lunch and change the contents, but proper labeling lets them know it's not the proper thing to do. The names of protected attributes start with a single underscore. Private attributes on the other hand are only accessible by the class and instances of the class. If a programmer tries to access the value from outside the class, they will receive an error. The names of private attributes start with two underscores.

Fun Fact

Private attributes are "name mangled" meaning that Python changes the format of the name so it is more difficult, but not impossible to access.

Public, Protected, and Private attributes

Commands
```
class MyClass:
    def __init__(self):
        self.public = "I am public"
        self._protected = "I am protected"
        self.__private = "I am private"

my_instance = MyClass()
print(my_instance.public)
print(my_instance._protected)
print(my_instance.__private)
```

Output
```
I am public
I am protected
Traceback (most recent call last):
  File "<string>", line 10, in <module>
AttributeError: 'MyClass' object has no attribute '__private'
```

To access and modify protected and private attributes, and for that matter public ones, we use methods that are commonly referred to as setters and getters. These are created the same as other methods, but it is convention to start the method name with get or set followed by an underscore and the name of the attribute. For example, if we had a protected attribute "birthday" we would want to write the methods .get_birthday() and .set_birthday() to access and modify the value.

If we were to write a class to handle bank accounts, we would want to avoid other programmers accessing and modifying our data in a way that we did not intend. In this banking example, we will want to use a number of public, protected, and private variables. In the example, we are choosing to have the email address remain public, protecting the name and account number, and making the balance and PIN private.

```python
class BankAccount:
    def __init__(self, acc_number, name, pin, email):
        self._account_number = acc_number
        self.__balance = 0
        self._name = name
        self.__pin = pin
        self.email = email

    def get_name(self):
        return self._name

    def set_name(self, new_name):
        self._name = new_name

    def get_pin(self):
        return self.__pin

    def set_pin(self, current_pin, new_pin):
        if current_pin == self.__pin:
            self.__pin = new_pin
            print("PIN updated successfully")
        else:
            print("Invalid PIN. Access denied")
```

In the example we use .get_name() and .set_name() to access and modify the account holder's name. We could write more complex code to verify the identity of the user before returning the account holder's name or to check validity of the name to set, but here we will keep things simple. In this example the name is only protected, so it can be modified directly, but programmers would know this is a bad idea based on the single underscore.

In regards to the PIN, `.get_pin()` simply returns the PIN, but `.set_pin()` requires the current PIN to also be entered correctly. Since the PIN is private, programmers cannot accidently change the PIN without going through the correct method. It can technically be modified, but it would have to be very intentional.

Using this class could look like this:

Commands

```
my_account = BankAccount(
    "123456", "Aurora Dawn", "1234", "aurora@email.com"
)
my_account.set_pin(1234, 5678)
print(my_account.get_pin())
```

Output

```
PIN updated successfully
5678
```

Trying to modify or access the PIN directly will result in an error.

Commands

```
my_account = BankAccount(
    "123456", "Aurora Dawn", "1234", "aurora@email.com"
)
print(my_account._pin())
```

Output

```
Traceback (most recent call last):
  File "<string>", line 27, in <module>
AttributeError: 'BankAccount' object has no attribute
'__pin'
```

If we try to assign a value to the private attribute __pin we might expect an error but instead we get some unexpected behavior. Python will create a new public attribute, however the getters and setters will still reference the correct, private attribute.

Commands

```
my_account = BankAccount(
    "123456", "Aurora Dawn", "1234", "aurora@email.com"
)
my_account.__pin = 5678
print("Improperly created PIN:", my_account.__pin)
print("Actual PIN:", my_account.get_pin())
```

Output

```
Improperly created PIN: 5678
Actual PIN: 1234
```

It is important to keep in mind that public, protected, and private attributes are more about informing programmers how much access they should have, preventing accidental modifications but they are not security measures since the information can still be intentionally accessed and modified.

5.6 Designing Object-Oriented Solutions

Coming from a procedural programming background may make the leap to object-oriented mindset appear challenging at first, but we are in luck. This new approach still starts with breaking complex problems down into smaller steps.

First, we must first identify the requirements of the program. For example, if we were writing software to handle daily operations in a restaurant, we might need to manage orders, track menu items, and handle staffing, among other things.

Once we identify our requirements, we should define the objects that we will need to create to handle these requirements. These are the main components that will need to interact in our system. For us, it makes sense to have a "MenuItem" class and an "Order" class. We would probably want a "Staff" class and a "Customer" class as well.

Once we understand our objects, we need to consider how they are related. This is where inheritance and composition come into play. If we have several similar objects, we could create a parent class that might handle the common details. If we have an object that would be very complex on its own, we might want to use composition to move some of the complexity into another class. For our restaurant program, "Order" might be made up of several "MenuItem" instances. "Staff" and "Customer" should inherit some of their attributes and methods from a common parent class, maybe a "Person" class.

Finally, we need to consider specific attributes and methods each individual class will need. This is where the actual coding of the classes will begin. Encapsulation needs to be considered as well to prevent our data from being accessed or modified in an unintended way. We need to consider how we can use getters and setters along with private, protected, and public attributes to protect values and to help abstract away the details of the objects. Our "MenuItem" class would need a "price" attribute, but we wouldn't want it to be modified by accident, so we would want to make it protected or private.

Simple versions of our classes are as follows.

```python
class MenuItem:
    def __init__(self, name, price, available):
        self.name = name
        self._price = price
        self._available = available

    def getPrice(self):
        return f"{self.name} costs ${self._price}"
```

In our "MenuItem" class, we are just storing information about the item. Since "self.price" is a protected attribute, we have a getter to return a string indicating the price. It wouldn't be hard to imagine modifying this class to handle sales, store ingredient information, and track orders.

```python
class Order:
  def __init__(self, order_id):
    self._order_id = order_id
    self._menu_items = []
    self._status = "Pending"

def add_item(self, menu_item):
  if menu_item._available:
    self._menu_items.append(menu_item)
    return f"Order {self._order_id}:Add {menu_item.name}."

def update_status(self, new_status):
  self._status = new_status
  return f"Order {self._order_id} status:{self._status}"
```

Orders may be made up of multiple items on the menu, so there should be a compositional relationship between our "Order" and "MenuItem" classes. In the add_item method, we can see that we pass in a menu_item and then store the instance in the protected attribute "self.order_id". We also have a method for updating the status of the order. Keeping everything neatly packaged this way makes for much more modular code which is easier to use and edit.

```python
class Person:
    def __init__(self, name, contact):
        self._name = name
        self._contact = contact
```

Our "Person" class is fairly simple, just taking in some basic information. The power comes from creating child classes with it.

```
class Staff(Person):
    def __init__(self, name, contact, staff_id):
        super().__init__(name, contact)
        self._staff_id = staff_id

    def manage_order(self, order, new_status):
        return order.update_status(new_status)
```

Our "Staff" class is a child of "Person". The parent class requires the name and contact, so we take those in as arguments. "Staff" also requires a staff ID, so that is passed in as well. The `super().__init__()` method is passed the name and contact because these are expected by the parent class. The "staff_id" is then set afterward in the constructor. We write the method for managing orders in the "Staff" class especially since it is only important for the staff and not other related classes.

```
class Customer(Person):
    def __init__(self, name, contact, customer_id):
    super().__init__(name, contact)
    self._customer_id = customer_id

    def place_order(self, order):
        return f"{self._name} placed order {self._order_id})"
```

Our "Customer" class is very similar, taking a "customer_id" instead of a "staff_id". There is a "place_order" method that is not in the "Staff" class since this is a behavior that would only be seen in customers.

Designing object-oriented solutions involves understanding the problem and thinking about it in terms of objects and relationships. Encapsulation, abstraction, inheritance, and polymorphism, work together to allow us to write modular code that is both flexible and maintainable.

Quiz

1. **Which keyword is used to define a class in Python?**
    a. class
    b. def
    c. function
    d. module

2. **Which illustrates the correct naming convention for class names in Python?**
    a. class playing_card
    b. class playingCard
    c. class PLAYING_CARD
    d. class PlayingCard

3. **What is "self"?**
    a. A reference to global variables
    b. A reference to local variables
    c. A reference to a class
    d. A reference to an instance of a class

4. **If there is a class "Car" which takes no arguments, which would create an instance of "Car"?**
    a. my_car = Car()
    b. my_car = Car(self)
    c. my_car = new Car()
    d. Car.my_car()

5. What is OOP?

a. Object Oriented Programming

b. Open Online Program

c. Overhead Objective Processing

d. Object Operation Procedure

6. Which method initializes an object in Python?

a. `__begin__`

b. `__create__`

c. `__init__`

d. `__start__`

7. Which defines composition?

a. Combining basic object to create more complex ones

b. Defining multiple classes within a single script

c. Inheriting from multiple classes

d. Overriding methods

8. What is the purpose of abstraction?

a. To reveal the inner workings of an object

b. To create private methods and hidden data

c. To conceal details and only display only what is necessary

d. To write less verbose code

9. Considering inheritance, which is true?

a. Inheritance allows a class to be created based on another class

b. Inheritance prevents code from being reused

c. Inheritance and polymorphism cannot be used together

d. Inheritance and composition are different names for the same concept

10. Which is an example of a private attribute?

   a. `self.apple`

   b. `self._banana`

   c. `self.__cherry`

   d. `self.#donut`

Answers	1 – a	2 – d	3 – d	4 – a	5 – a
	6 – c	7 – a	8 – c	9 – a	10 – c

Chapter Summary

◆ Classes contain attributes and methods used to create the objects, known as instances.

◆ We can relate different classes to help write reusable code by using concepts such as inheritance and composition.

◆ Polymorphism allows classes to be expanded and allows for complex relationships.

◆ It is best practice to encapsulate classes, limiting data access from within classes.

This page is intentionally left blank

Chapter **6**

Error Handling and Exceptions

In this chapter we investigate the frustrating, yet important world of errors and exceptions. While it may initially feel like learning another foreign language, errors quickly become a helpful tool that Python uses to inform us about problems in our code. We will go beyond letting Python tell us what errors are occurring and move toward setting up our own error situations and writing our own custom errors.

The key learning objectives of this chapter are:

- Understanding the information being given in an error report

- Understanding some of the basic error types

- Using try-except blocks to handle errors without crashes

- Raising exceptions in problem situations

- Writing custom exceptions when built-in functions are not suitable

6.1 Understanding Errors and Exceptions

As we have been writing programs, we have encountered various errors and feedback information. While it is annoying when we cannot track down the source of an error, Python provides us with useful information that we can use to help determine what is this issue, and versions 3.11 and higher have even more descriptive error messages than previous versions.[12]

Broadly speaking, there are three major types of errors, but we will break them down in more detail later in this section.

- **Syntax errors:** Occur when we go against the syntax rules of Python. These errors are reported before the program executes and prevents the program from running at all. These are the simplest to detect.

- **Runtime errors:** Occur while the program is running. These halt the program's execution when the line of code is reached. These can be easier to miss when working on large projects.

- **Logical errors:** Occur while the program is running. These do not stop the program and do not produce an error

---

12. Python Documentation, "What's New in Python 3.11 – Python 3.11.8 documentation" accessed June 23, 2024, https://docs.python.org/3.11/whatsnew/3.11. html

message, but produce incorrect results. These can be the hardest to track down since the program will continue as normal.

Having our programs stop whenever there is an error may seem like a major annoyance, and it is certainly a source of frustration, but it is a necessary behavior. For programmers having programs stop with information provided makes debugging much simpler. Having the program stop gives us a clue as to what triggered the error in the first place. For the end user, having an error stop the program will prevent unintended consequences such as deleted data, incorrect communication, or even hardware errors. We wouldn't want the end user to experience these errors, as we should thoroughly test our program, but at least we can prevent the program from doing something unsafe. The user would also receive the error message which they could report back to us, giving us a way of addressing the issue in a future update.

When error messages are produced, we can expect several pieces of information to help us track down the source of the error. We get the error type and a description of the error, along with the file name and line number to help us find the error. We also receive a *traceback* which shows the sequence of *function* calls that led to the error in the first place. Often it is not the line where the error occurred that is the issue, but where the information came from that is the issue. We also may receive a sample of the code that caused the error giving us more context for the error.

Here is a sample program with two errors.

Commands

```
def greet(name)
    print("Hello, " + Name)

greet("Locklynn")
```

Output

```
Traceback (most recent call last):
  File "C:\python\main.py", line 1
    def greet(name)
                   ^
SyntaxError: expected ':'
```

Here we have forgotten the colon at the end of our function declaration. This syntax error prevents the program from running at all as Python doesn't know how to handle the improper function definition. In the error message we can see that the error occurred in the "main.py" file on line 1. We also can see the coding context with a helpful arrow pointing at the error. We can also see that it is a syntax error and that it has been caused by the lack of a colon. The traceback in this case is just the first line since nothing actually ran.

If we fix this issue, we get another error.

Commands

```
def greet(name):
    print("Hello, " + Name)

greet("Locklynn")
```

Output

```
Traceback (most recent call last):
  File "C:\python\main.py", line 4, in <module>
    greet("Locklynn")
  File "C:\python\main.py", line 2, in greet
    print("Hello, " + Name)
NameError: name 'Name' is not defined
```

This one is a runtime error due to a NameError. We capitalized "Name" within the function and since Python is case sensitive, "Name" is not defined. This is easy to fix; we just need to change it to "name".

Analyzing the output, we can see that the traceback is a little more complicated. The error starts with our function call, greet("Locklynn"). This occurs on line 4 in the main file. We can see that the error then continues on line 2, inside the `greet()` function where the actual error occurs. In this case there is no handy arrow to indicate where the error is, but the error description tells us very plainly that "Name" is not defined. Depending on your programming environment, you might even get an even more helpful message "NameError: name 'Name' is not defined. Did you mean: 'name'?"

In Python, errors are represented by a BaseException class which interrupts the program by raising the exception. Each type of error is represented by its own child class of BaseException which, as discussed in Chapter 5, means they inherit the methods while allowing for their own methods to be added or overridden. We will use this to write our own custom exceptions later in the chapter. Some common types of exceptions are shown in Table 6.1.[13]

---

13. Python Documentation "Built-in Exceptions – Python 3.12.4", accessed June 29 2024, https://docs.python.org/3/library/exceptions.html

Table 6.1	**Common Exceptions**
SyntaxError	Occurs when code is not written following Python's syntax rules.
TypeError	Occurs when a function is applied to the wrong type of value.
ValueError	Occurs when a function receives an argument with an inappropriate value.
ZeroDivisionError	Occurs when a number is divided by zero.
IndexError	Occurs when an index is used that is out of range for a sequence.

There are far too many types of exceptions to list them all, but the names of the exceptions along with the additional information provided should give us enough information to determine how to address the issue.

Commands

```python
def calculate_total(prices, tax_rate):
    total = 0
    for price in prices:
        total += price

    tax = total * tax_rate
        total_with_tax = total + tax

    return total_with_tax

prices = [10.99, 20.49, 3.50]
tax_rate = 0.07
total = calculate_total(prices, tax_rate)
print(f"Total with tax: ${round(total,2)}")
```

Output

```
Traceback (most recent call last):
  File "C:\python\main.py", line 7
    total_with_tax = total + tax
IndentationError: unexpected indent
```

In this example, we can see that an IndentationError has been raised. Since Python tends to be descriptive, we can assume that there is a problem with the indentation in our program. There is extra information provided that tells us that there is an unexpected indent. The traceback lets us see that the cause is line 7, and looking at the code, we can see there is indeed an extra indent on line 7.

Before we look at how to handle these exceptions, a word of caution. When working with imported modules the traceback can get quite lengthy and potentially confusing. The following code shows a short example of this behavior, but the traceback can be pages long.

Exception involving the random library

Commands

```
from random import choice

favorite_movies = []
movie_to_watch = choice(favorite_movies)
print(f"You should watch {movie_to_watch}")
```

Output

```
Traceback (most recent call last):
  File "C:\python\main.py", line 4, in <module>
    movie_to_watch = choice(favorite_movies)
  File "C:\AppData\Local\Programs\Python\Python312\lib\
random.py", line 378, in choice
    return seq[self._randbelow(len(seq))]
IndexError: list index out of range
```

We see the same information that we would normally expect, however we can see a different file path and an extremely high line number. How can we have an error on line 378 if our script is only 5 lines long? How can we have an *IndexError* when we didn't try to use an index?

If we analyze the traceback, we can see the error started on line 4 in the `main.py` file where we tried to use the `choice()` function from the random library. Following that, we can see that the next issue was in a `random.py` file stored in a different location. All of our libraries, including built-in Python libraries, have to be stored somewhere on our computers and they tend to be stored with the installation of Python. We can open this file in our Python IDE to investigate further, but this is where many programmers would simply perform a search for the error online. Sites like Stack Overflow can be an excellent resource to search for similar problems, or to create a post to ask about the issue. Many code editors now also come bundled with AI tools which help to analyze potential errors.

We can use the file address to investigate the `random.py` file directly. We can see from lines 375 to 378:

```
def choice(self, seq):
    """Choose a random element from a non-empty
sequence."""
    # raises IndexError if seq is empty
    return seq[self._randbelow(len(seq))]
```

We can see that our empty *list* caused the index error. If we populate the list with our favorite movies the program will run as expected.

When dealing with lengthy tracebacks, it would be a good idea to investigate the first and last piece as this is where the error was initiated and where it finally occurred.

6.2 Handling Errors with Try-Except Blocks

Exceptions are going to happen in our code. Even if we pay close attention to detail and consider all possibilities, other programmers and end users are going to try something that we did not anticipate. We may not be able to completely avoid errors, but we can help our programs handle these exceptions gracefully. We use *try-except* blocks for this task. Try-except blocks are written similar to if-then blocks with code indented to indicate which parts of the code we want to execute depending on if there is an error or not.

The syntax is as follows:

```
try:
    #code that might case an exception
except:
    #code that catches the exception
finally:
    #code that runs regardless
```

There are many situations where we might use this structure. If we want to open a file, that file might not exist. If we are dividing numbers, the potential for the divisor to be zero may exist. If we ask a user to enter a number, they may write it out in words instead of digits.

Handling exceptions allows us to prevent our programs from stopping when a problem situation occurs, leading to a better experience for the end user. It also can be used to give descriptive feedback to us, and help other programmers with debugging and maintenance of code.

It is easier to understand this through examples rather than just from an academic discussion, so let us investigate a simple division calculator as seen in the following code:

Simple division calculator

```
print("Please enter 2 numbers to divide")
num1 = float(input("Number 1: "))
num2 = float(input("Number 2: "))
print(f"{num1} divided by {num2} is {num1/num2}")
```

There is so much potential for exceptions here. Since we are using the float function to convert the *string* entered into a *float* we would get an error if the user enters a non-numerical value. Since there is division, we also have the potential for the user to enter a zero as the second number, raising a ZeroDivisionError.

User Input		Output
Num1	Num2	
10	5	10.0 divided by 5.0 is 2.0
ten	5	Traceback (most recent call last): File "C:\python\main.py", line 2, in <module> num1 = float(input("Number 1: ")) ValueError: could not convert string to float: 'ten'
10	0	Traceback (most recent call last): File "C:\python\main.py", line 4, in <module> print(f"{num1} divided by {num2} is {num1/num2}") ZeroDivisionError: float division by zero

To address these issues, we can use a try-except block.

```
try:
    print("Please enter 2 numbers to divide")
    num1 = float(input("Number 1: "))
    num2 = float(input("Number 2: "))
    print(f"{num1} divided by {num2} is {num1/num2}")
except:
    print("You entered an incorrect value")
```

Now we can run our program without the fear of it crashing, however the feedback only tells us that there is an incorrect value. It would be much better if we had some information about the error.

User Input		Output
Num1	Num2	
10	5	10.0 divided by 5.0 is 2.0
ten	5	You entered an incorrect value
10	0	You entered an incorrect value

This is somewhat like when we use an `if` statement to run a piece of code if the condition is true and an `else` statement to catch everything else. With if-then blocks, we can also use the `elif` statement to add additional conditions. There is no `elif` with try-except blocks, but we can use multiple "excepts" with a specific exception type. This makes different code run based on which exception was raised.

Here is the final version of the code:

```python
try:
    print("Please enter 2 numbers to divide")
    num1 = float(input("Number 1: "))
    num2 = float(input("Number 2: "))
    print(f"{num1} divided by {num2} is {num1/num2}")
except ValueError:
    print("You need to enter a numerical value")
except ZeroDivisionError:
    print("You cannot divide by zero")
except:
    print("You entered an incorrect value")
    print(num1,num2, "were entered")
```

User Input		Output
Num1	Num2	
10	5	10.0 divided by 5.0 is 2.0
ten	5	You need to enter a numerical value
10	0	You cannot divide by zero

Our *"ValueError"* and *"ZeroDivisionError"* should catch all the exceptions, but it is still a good idea to have a final except statement to catch anything we didn't expect. This prevents our program from crashing and could be useful for debugging purposes.

If we want to get the specific information from Python, we can add the "as" keyword to our exceptions. By convention, we typically use the *variable* "e" to stand in for the error, but it can be any valid variable name.

```
try:
    print("Please enter 2 numbers to divide")
    num1 = float(input("Number 1: "))
    num2 = float(input("Number 2: "))
    print(f"{num1} divided by {num2} is {num1/num2}")
except ValueError as e:
    print("You need to enter a numerical value.")
    print(f"Specific error:{e}")
except ZeroDivisionError as e:
    print("You cannot divide by zero.")
    print(f"Specific error:{e}")
except:
    print("You entered an incorrect value")
    print(num1,num2, "were entered")
```

User Input		Output
Num1	Num2	
10	5	10.0 divided by 5.0 is 2.0
ten	5	You need to enter a numerical value. Specific error:could not convert string to float: 'ten'
10	0	You cannot divide by zero. Specific error:float division by zero

Using the keyword *"finally"* is something that is optional in most cases, but it is often used to encapsulate the logic of an operation within the try-except block. While the code inside the "finally" block can usually be written after the try-except statement is complete, including it as part of the exception handling can make the code cleaner and easier to read.

While we have not been opening and reading files yet, we will look into this in more detail in Chapter 7 so we won't worry about the details here. For now, we should understand that if we open a file, we should also close it.

```
file_path = "missing.txt"
file = None
try:
    print("Opening the file...")
    file = open(file_path, 'r')
    content = file.read()
    print(f"File content: {content}")

except FileNotFoundError:
    print("The file does not exist.")
except ValueError:
    print("There is an error with the file contents.")
except:
    print("An unexpected error occurred.")
finally:
    if file:
        print("Closing the file...")
        file.close()
```

When trying to read a file there are many errors that could occur. The most obvious is that the file might not exist. There could also be issues with the contents of the file, or something unexpected could occur. This is why there is an "except FileNotFoundError", an "except ValueError", and a generic "except". With all these issues, there is a possibility that we open the file but an error could interrupt the normal flow of the program before we get a chance to close it. In the "finally" block, we check if the file was opened before and close it if necessary. This keeps the logic contained to one block, making everything a little more readable. Adding "finally" to the end of a try-except block is not a tool that we will use frequently, however it is still a useful technique to be aware of, especially when there is some kind of clean up, such as closing a file, after handling exceptions.

6.3 Raising and Handling Custom Exceptions

As programmers we have a lot of control in the code that we write. Rather than waiting for Python to detect an error, we can tell Python that an error is going to occur. We call this raising an exception.

For example, we looked at how to make sure a key is present in a *dictionary* before accessing or modifying the value using the "in" keyword. Failure to do so could result in a *key error*. Using a slightly modified example from chapter 3, we can rewrite it to use a try-except block.

Original Code

```
sale_items = {'chair': 50, 'art': 200, 'book': 10}
if "book" in sale_items:
    price = sale_items.pop("book")
    print("That will be $",price, sep = "")
else:
    print("We don't have a book")
```

Try-Except Version

```
sale_items = {'chair': 50, 'art': 200, 'book': 10}
try:
    price = sale_items.pop("book")
    print("That will be $",price, sep = "")
except KeyError:
    print("We don't have a book")
except:
    print("Unknown error")
```

We'll take this one step further which might seem like a strange example but will aptly illustrate a few points. What if our house ended up in the sale_items dictionary by accident? The "raise" keyword can be used to force an error to occur. The syntax is the "raise" keyword followed by the type of error.

To ensure our house doesn't accidently get sold we will have to check if the item requested is a house. If the item is a house, we can "raise KeyError". This forces a key error to be called regardless of whether there is a house in the dictionary of items for sale.

```python
sale_items = {
    'chair': 50, 'art': 200,
    'book': 10, 'house':100000
    }

def purchase_item(item_name):

    try:
        if item_name == 'house':
            raise KeyError
        price = sale_items.pop(item_name)
        print(f"Price of {item_name}: ${price}")
    except KeyError:
        print(f"We don't have a {item_name} for sale")
    except Exception as e:
        print(f"Unknown error: {e}")

item_to_buy = input("Enter item to purchase: ")
purchase_item(item_to_buy)
```

But how could our house end up in our dictionary of sale items? Keep in mind that programming is not a solo event. Other people could be working on our code or could use our code as a basis for developing their own programs, so it is possible that the values could be changed.

In this case, it makes sense to use the built-in error "KeyError" because we are trying to access a key that we really shouldn't be accessing. Typically, key errors are raised when a key is not found in a dictionary, but this isn't much of a logical stretch to understand the connection. While any error could be used, it wouldn't make sense to raise a FileNotFoundError or DivisionByZeroError since they are unrelated to what we are trying to catch with our exception handling.

If we have a situation where we are unsure of the best exception to use, we have two main options: raising "Exception", which is the basic exception type, or writing a custom exception. Let's imagine we are setting up a ticketing system where we want to restrict people under 18 from buying tickets. While we could raise a value error, it doesn't really convey the meaning we are trying to express.

When raising an exception, you can pass in additional information to display. This can be done with any exception type if we want to provide extra information. This information can be accessed through the variable we pair with the "as" keyword, typically "e".

Commands
```
age = 16
try:
    if age < 18:
        raise Exception("You are too young")
except Exception as e:
    print(e)
```

Output
```
You are too young
```

Instead of using this generic error, we can create a custom InvalidAgeError. As a bare minimum, we can create a child class of Exception and just write "pass" in the body of the class. This allows us to leave it blank without triggering an indentation error. The code looks essentially the same, but the meaning is clearer.

Commands

```
class InvalidAgeError(Exception):
    pass

age = 16
try:
    if age < 18:
        raise InvalidAgeError("You are too young")
except InvalidAgeError as e:
    print(e)
```

Output

```
You are too young
```

It might seem strange to go through all of this work when a simple if statement would perform the same task, but if statements are not as modular. By setting up our error once, we can reuse it in different situations in our code. We could also take all of our custom errors and store them in a separate file like when we looked at functions and classes.

There may be several times where we want to check a person's age. By using our custom error, we can eliminate some of the repetition required for multiple if statements.

Commands

```python
class InvalidAgeError(Exception):
  pass

def check_age_for_movie(age):
  if age < 18:
    raise InvalidAgeError("Too young to buy tickets.")
  print("You can buy movie tickets.")

def check_age_for_alcohol(age):
  if age < 21:
    raise InvalidAgeError("Too young to buy alcohol.")
  print("You can buy alcohol.")

def check_age_for_renting_car(age):
  if age < 25:
    raise InvalidAgeError("Too young to rent a car.")
  print("You can rent a car.")

age = 20
try:
  check_age_for_movie(age)
  check_age_for_alcohol(age)
  check_age_for_renting_car(age)
except InvalidAgeError as e:
  print(e)
finally:
  print(f"It must be nice being {age}!")
```

Output

```
You can buy movie tickets.
Too young to buy alcohol.
It must be nice being 20!
```

Here we try to execute all three of our functions and check for age errors. If an age error occurs, we print the message associated with that specific error instance. When we wrap multiple lines of code in a single try statement like this, any lines after an error will not run. This is why there is no message about renting a car, since that function is never called. This can be intentional such as giving a list of privileges, but it may not always be what we want to occur. This might not be the most efficient way to ensure each function was called as we would need a try-except block for each function call.

Not only does using custom exceptions in this way helps with reusability, but also allows us to provide clear and specific error messages. We can also use this technique to keep our error handling separate from the rest of our program. This makes things cleaner and more maintainable, especially when other programmers or users start interacting with our code.

Quiz

1. **Which type of error is the most difficult to detect?**
   a. Logical errors
   b. Index errors
   c. Runtime errors
   d. Syntax errors

2. **Which type of error prevents programs from running at all?**
   a. Logical errors
   b. Index errors
   c. Runtime errors
   d. Syntax errors

3. **What type of error would be raised when this code is run?**

```
for i in range(5):
        print(i)
```

   a. IndentationError
   b. IndexError
   c. TracebackError
   d. TypeError

4. If this code is run, what would be the output?

```
try:
    print("Sun")
finally:
    print("Moon")
```

a. Sun

b. Moon

c. Sun
   Moon

d. There is an error

5. What is the purpose of the "except" block in a try-except statement?

a. Defines the logic of the error

b. Executes regardless of an error

c. Executes only if there is no error

d. Executes only if there is an error

6. Which code snippet would not raise an exception?

a.	`int('abc')`
b.	`5/0`
c.	`my_list = [1,2,3,4]` `print(my_list[4])`
d.	`my_dict = {"name":"Tim","age":28}` `print(my_dict["name"])`

7. What is a "traceback"?

a. A list of all variables defined

b. An error message with extra details

c. sequence of function calls leading to an error

d. A key log leading up to the error

8. **What type of error is raised by the code?**

```
my_list = [1,2,3]
item = my_list[5]
```

   a. TypeError
   b. IndexError
   c. KeyError
   d. ValueError

9. **What type of exception would be raised if a value is divided by zero?**
   a. SyntaxError
   b. TypeError
   c. ValueError
   d. ZeroDivisionError

10. **Why is exception handling important?**
   a. To code run faster
   b. To handle runtime errors gracefully
   c. To fix syntax errors
   d. To replace if-then blocks

Answers	1 – a	2 – d	3 – a	4 – c	5 – d
	6 – d	7 – c	8 – b	9 – d	10 – b

Chapter Summary

◆ Errors are reported by Python in such a way that it helps us track down the source of the error.

◆ "Try" blocks attempt to run code that could cause an error while "expect" blocks contain code that runs if there is an error.

◆ Finally blocks contain "clean up" code that runs regardless of the try-except section.

◆ Exceptions can be raised in situations that would not typically cause an error by using the "raise" keyword.

◆ Custom errors can be created to make error messages more meaningful in the context of our programs

Chapter **7**

A Practical Guide for Working Professionals

In this chapter we will investigate the world of data and how understanding the basics of working with data using Python can help improve employability. Pandas and Matplotlib will be two key libraries used to analyze data and create graphs and charts to visualize our data

The key learning objectives of this chapter are:

- Understanding the importance of data in making decisions

- Loading, cleaning, and analyzing data with Pandas

- Creating visualizations with Matplotlib

7.1 The Role of Data in Today's Workplace

In today's workplace, data is one of the most important assets for making informed decisions. We could even say that data is the new oil. Every click, swipe, and interaction that we engage in can be harvested by companies to gain insight into how we interact with their services.

Regardless of your industry, data is the driving force behind the strategies that businesses use to gain a competitive edge. According to the World Economic Forum, more than 75% of businesses intend to incorporate big data, AI, and cloud computing into their business models. Digital platforms and apps are also expected to be incorporated into most businesses.[14] Apps are an excellent way for companies to collect data about their customers, but the amount of data collected is too great to be managed traditionally, so we turn to *big data*. Big data is a series of tools and techniques that are used to glean insight from massive, varied datasets. The vast volume of data is too complex to be processed using traditional methods. Much of this data needs to be stored and analyzed in "the cloud", which essentially means it is stored on someone else's computer that is connected to the internet rather than your local computer. Often companies will use services such as Amazon Web Services (AWS), Microsoft Azure, or Google Cloud Platform to handle this large amount of data.

Where does AI come in? Artificial Intelligence is a huge buzzword these days, and as Figure 7.1 shows, it is at the peak of its worldwide interest level.

---

14. World Economic Forum, "Future of Jobs Report 2023 – Insight Report May 2023", published April 30, 2023, https://www3.weforum.org/docs/WEF_Future_of_Jobs_2023. pdf

Figure 7.1 **Worldwide Interest in the Search Term "AI"**

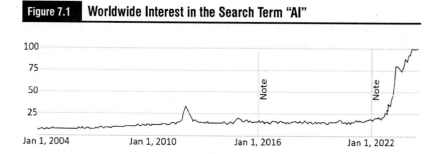

Data source: Google Trends, accessed June 30, 2024 (https://www.google.com/trends)

Using *artificial intelligence* is one method of analyzing all of this data. Using AI, especially *machine learning based on statistics,* we can identify patterns and make predictions that would be impossible to achieve using traditional techniques. We will investigate these concepts in detail in Chapter 9.

Netflix, for example, uses user data to not only recommend content to users, it also uses the information to determine how to advertise these shows to different users, targeting them with ads that match up with their demographics and viewing habits.[15] Likewise, Starbucks uses its app data to determine new beverage options based on user's preferences, but it also tracks individual user's behaviors to offer specialized offers to increase sales.[16] Whichever industry we explore, there is room for improvement with faster, more localized, data analytics. It could be fraud detection and credit risk analysis in finance, or predictive diagnostics and personalized treatment plans in the healthcare industry.

---

15. Vartan Pahalyants, "Netflix: A Streaming Gian's Big Data Approach to Entertainment", accessed June 30, 2024, https://d3.harvard.edu/platform-digit/submission/netflix-a-streaming-giants-big-data-approach-to-entertainment/

16. Stéphane V, "Starbucks: From Coffee Machines to Machine Learning", accessed June 30, 2024, https://d3.harvard.edu/platform-digit/submission/starbucks-from-coffee-machines-to-machine-learning/

However, technology is a double-edged sword and when we look at data, we need to be careful of how it is being collected and used. There are many ethical concerns that need to be considered when dealing with user data. The best practice is to be transparent, accountable, and respectful of user privacy. If we plan on using user data to offer targeted ads, we need to ensure that users are aware and agree to this practice. It is also important to minimize the amount of data that we collect. We should only collect and store information related to the specific purpose. If we want to determine what ads to show a user, we would want some demographic information and purchase history, but we wouldn't need to track location data or payment methods. Minimizing the amount of data we collect helps reduce the risk of the data being misused within a business, or in the event of a data breach, by hackers. Wherever possible, data should be stored in a way that is as anonymous as possible to minimize the damage done by a potential breach.

Not only is this a good practice, but there are also regulations for various industries that determine how and what we can collect and store. While there are many different regulatory bodies, some common regulations include the individual's right to access their own data and have it deleted upon request. Also common to regulations is the right to opt out from data use. In the event of a data breach, regulations need to be included about how to notify users and the timeframe for doing so.[17][18]

---

17. European Parliament and Council of the European Union. *Regulation (EU) 2016/679 of the European Parliament and of the Council of 27 April 2016 on the Protection of Natural Persons with regard to the Processing of Personal Data and on the Free Movement of Such Data, and Repealing Directive 95/46/EC (General Data Protection Regulation).* Official Journal of the European Union L 119/1, May 4, 2016, accessed June 29, 2024, https://eur-lex.europa.eu/legal-content/EN/TXT/PDF/?uri=CELEX:32016R0679.

18. California State Legislature, *California Consumer Privacy Act of 2018,* California Civil Code, Division 3, Part 4, Title 1.81.5. Accessed June 29, 2024. https://leginfo.legislature.ca.gov/faces/codes_displayText.xhtml?division=3.&part=4.&lawCode=CIV&title=1.81.5.

Data is a critical part of business, but it's also important to understand and implement ethical and compliant data practices. This allows us to use data to gain insights and improve our business models but also protects user data and helps build trust among consumers. Otherwise, we could end up in the midst of a scandal as Facebook did in 2018 when millions of user's data was used for political advertising without consent.[19] When customers feel that they have been betrayed or misled, it is difficult, if not impossible, to gain that trust back.

7.2 Navigating Data Analytics

7.2.1 Loading Data

When we examine a set of data to draw meaningful conclusions about the information, we call this data analytics. As discussed in the previous section, this is a data driven world, and we might want to use data in a number of different ways which could include optimizing operations, enhancing customer experiences, and driving innovation. Regardless of our goal, we must first have a way of storing our data. Table 7.1 shows several different formats for storing data, but we will focus on *CSV files* due to their simplicity and easy usability.

---

19. Carole Cadwalladr and Emma Graham-Harrison, "Revealed: 50 Million Facebook Profiles Harvested for Cambridge Analytica in Major Data Breach," *The Guardian*, March 17, 2018, https://www.theguardian.com/news/2018/mar/17/cambridge-analytica-facebook-influence-us-election.

Table 7.1   **Various file formats for storing data**

Format	Description	Use Case	Advantage	Disadvantages
CSV (*.csv)	Comma-Separated Values, a simple text-based format for tabular data	Simple storage and file transfer	Widely supported and easy to use.	Limited support for complex data.
JSON (*.json)	JavaScript Object Notation, a lightweight data format	Web applications and API	Great for connected data.	Less readable for large datasets.
XML (*.xml)	Extensible Markup Language, a way of storing structured data using markup language	Document storage and data exchange	Supports complex data structures.	Can be slow to process.
Excel (*.xlsx)	Microsoft's spreadsheet format, supports complex data manipulation	Data analysis and reporting	Easy to use with data analysis using built-in functions.	Requires specific software to use.
SQL (*.sql)	Structured Query Language, used for relational databases	Data management	Efficient for large datasets with complex relationships.	Requires knowledge of SQL and databases.

First of all, what is a CSV file? CSV stands for comma-separated values and contains information in a table setup. The file itself just contains text information with the cell values separated by commas, colons, spaces, pipes, or tabs, and the end of a row marked with a hard return. The first row may contain the headings for the columns. Figure 7.2 shows what a CSV file could look like if you opened it with a text editor, although if you use a spreadsheet program to open one, the formatting will be organized into a spreadsheet format.

Figure 7.2	**The content of a CSV file with the first row as heading**

```
ID,Name,Age,Salary,Department
1,Akira,35,75000,HR
2,Sophia,42,92000,Finance
3,Aaron,28,61000,IT
4,Liam,54,115000,Sales
5,Priyanka,23,45000,Marketing
```

The formatting of this leaves a lot to be desired, but we tend not to read the files directly, and instead rely on Python to help us with the data.

There are a variety of methods to load CSV data into our Python scripts but the most efficient is to use the Pandas library. Pandas is a powerful and flexible Python library designed for analyzing and manipulating data. It is not built into Python, so we need to install it. We discussed installing libraries using pip in Chapter 4. If you are working locally on your computer, you will need to use your command prompt to enter the command "pip install pandas", but if you are working with an online IDE, it will likely install it for you or there may be an option to enable it. Pandas is a very popular library for working with data so it will be supported by most online IDEs. Typically, when people import Pandas, they use the statement "import pandas as pd" to minimize the length of the statements that have to be written. This doesn't have to be done, but it is the standard convention and is best to do out of consistency.

To work with Pandas, we first need a *dataset*. Businesses tend to generate their own data, but there is also a wealth of information available online as well. We will be working with data from data. gov. The data is available for free without having to sign up for an account, and for the most part, it can be used without restriction, although non-federal data sometimes falls under a different license.[20] The "Licensed Drivers, by state, gender, and age group" dataset, available at https://catalog.data.gov/dataset/licensed-drivers-by-state-gender-and-age-group will be our initial dataset. Most online IDEs will allow small files to be uploaded to the main project folder. When using Python on a local machine, be careful of where you save the file. To make it easier to access our data, we will save our dataset in the same folder as our main Python file, but keep in mind that with more complex projects it is common to have data stored in a subfolder.

Once we have our data in the right place, we want to be able to open it. Pandas has two main data structures, *Series* and *DataFrame*. A Series is similar to the built-in lists in Python and represents a single column of data. A DataFrame is like an entire table and will be our main focus. It is common practice to use the *variable* "df" to represent a DataFrame, but it may be more appropriate to use a more descriptive variable name to represent the table data.

To load a CSV into a DataFrame, we use the `read_csv()` function of the Pandas module. It takes the relative file path of the CSV file as the argument. This is why it is best for us to keep our file in the same location as our Python script so we can just refer to it by filename. Remember we will use the "as" keyword to rename pandas to pd, but this is optional as shown in Table 7.2.

---

20. Data.gov, "Privacy and Website Policies", accessed July 2, 2024, https://data.gov/privacy-policy/

Table 7.2	Reading a CSV with and without "as"
No "as"	```Import pandas
df = pandas.read_csv("Licensed_Drivers__by_
state__gender__and_age_group.csv")```
"as pd"	```import pandas as pd
df = pd.read_csv("Licensed_Drivers__by_state__
gender__and_age_group.csv")```

7.2.2 Understanding Data

Once the data is loaded, we will want a preview of our data. Since most datasets are quite large, Pandas DataFrames have a "head" and "tail" method that shows just the beginning and end of the data, respectively. We can pass in a specific number of entries, but if we leave it blank, we will get five.

`print(df.head())`	Year	Gender	Cohort	State	Drivers
	0 2017	Male	Under 16	Alabama	0.0
	1 2017	Male	Under 16	Alaska	0.0
	2 2017	Male	Under 16	Arizona	0.0
	3 2017	Male	Under 16	Arkansas	0.0
	4 2017	Male	Under 16	California	0.0
`print(df.head(3))`	Year	Gender	Cohort	State	Drivers
	0 2017	Male	Under 16	Alabama	0.0
	1 2017	Male	Under 16	Alaska	0.0
	2 2017	Male	Under 16	Arizona	0.0
`print(df.tail())`		Year	Gender	Cohort	State	Drivers
	57829	2018	Female	65-69	Wyoming	16061.0
	57830	2018	Female	70-74	Wyoming	11804.0
	57831	2018	Female	75-79	Wyoming	7770.0
	57832	2018	Female	80-84	Wyoming	4715.0
	57833	2018	Female	85+	Wyoming	3456.0

This gives us an idea of the data without having to read through all the data. We can see that we have columns that represent the year, gender, and state of the drivers. The ages are not provided as integers, but rather as a range of values, and we have a total number of drivers as well. Knowing this can give us a starting point for working with our data.

To get a little more information, we can use the `.info()` and `.describe()` methods on our DataFrame. The `.info()` method tells us how many columns we have, along with their headings. It also provides a "non-null" count, indicating how many entries are not blank and the data type of each column. Most of the data types should look familiar, but Pandas classifies strings as objects, which can cause some confusion. Another odd behavior is that we do not need to use the `print()` function to display the information from `.info()`. It is automatically printed to the console.

The `.describe()` method is a little more mathematical and only displays information on numerical columns and provides information useful for statistics. Most useful for us are the mean, minimum value, and maximum value, but information is also provided on the standard deviation and the quartiles, giving us a good idea of the variation and clustering of our data.

One other detail for non-mathematically minded readers: if we are dealing with data containing large numbers or small decimal numbers, Pandas will default to scientific notation. While extremely useful, scientific notation can be confusing for some people. To change this behavior, we can put this line "`pd.set_option('display.float_format', '{:.2f}'.format)`" near the beginning of our code before we print out any information to make the output more accessible, forcing the output to two decimal places. For example 0.0125 would be displayed as 0.01.

df.info()	```<class 'pandas.core.frame.DataFrame'>```
	```RangeIndex: 57834 entries, 0 to 57833```
	```Data columns (total 5 columns):```
	``` # Column Non-Null Count Dtype```
	```--- ------ -------------- -----```
	``` 0 Year 57834 non-null int64```
	``` 1 Gender 57834 non-null object```
	``` 2 Cohort 57834 non-null object```
	``` 3 State 57834 non-null object```
	``` 4 Drivers 57833 non-null float64```
	```dtypes: float64(1), int64(1), object(3)```
	```memory usage: 2.2+ MB```
print(df.describe())	``` Year Drivers```
	```count 57834.000000 5.783300e+04```
	```mean 2006.155203 8.708183e+04```
	```std 7.141656 1.412310e+05```
	```min 1994.000000 0.000000e+00```
	```25% 2000.000000 1.458200e+04```
	```50% 2006.000000 3.558400e+04```
	```75% 2012.000000 9.784800e+04```
	```max 2018.000000 1.417096e+06```
pd.set_option('display.float_format', '{:.2f}'.format) print(df.describe())	``` Year Drivers```
	```count 57834.00 57833.00```
	```mean 2006.16 87081.83```
	```std 7.14 141231.00```
	```min 1994.00 0.00```
	```25% 2000.00 14582.00```
	```50% 2006.00 35584.00```
	```75% 2012.00 97848.00```
	```max 2018.00 1417096.00```

Some interesting things to note here is the fact that there seems to be a single missing driver (57833 vs 57834) and that while we have a large data set, a lot of the information is from past years. Our next step will be to clean our data so that it has no missing data and only represents the most recent year.

7.2.3 Cleaning Data

We can check for missing, or *null*, values indirectly using the .info() method, but a simpler way to do so is to use the .isnull() method and sum the values. .isnull() returns a two dimensional array of True and False values which is not overly helpful on its own, but applying the `.sum()` method to this array, will give a total for each column.

`print(df.isnull())`	Year	Gender	Cohort	State	Drivers
	0 False	False	False	False	False
	1 False	False	False	False	False
	2 False	False	False	False	False
	3 False	False	False	False	False
	4 False	False	False	False	False
	...	...	...	...	...
	57829 False	False	False	False	False
	57830 False	False	False	False	False
	57831 False	False	False	False	False
	57832 False	False	False	False	False
	57833 False	False	False	False	False
	[57834 rows x 5 columns]				
`print(df.isnull().sum())`	Year 0				
	Gender 0				
	Cohort 0				
	State 0				
	Drivers 1				
	dtype: int64				

Once we identify that there are missing values, we need to determine how to handle it. One option is to fill the missing

values with a placeholder, often a zero. We can do this with the
.fillna() method, which takes the placeholder value as an
argument and has an optional argument, "inplace", which is False
by default. Using "inplace" can result in issues if we are making
multiple changes to our data, so it is best to avoid it. Table 7.3
shows a selection of ways that we can update our DataFrame with
the filled values.

Table 7.3	Methods of filling null values in a DataFrame
Reassign to the same variable	`df = df.fillna(0)`
Assign to a new variable	`newdf = df.fillna(0)`
Modify in place	`df.fillna(0, inplace=True)`

There are times when filling in the data could produce
inaccurate results, especially when there is a lot of missing data.
It may be best to simply remove any rows with missing data. To
do so, we simply use the .dropna() method. It is handled the
same way as the .fillna() method, but only takes the optional
"inplace" argument.

Dropping versus filling is really something that depends on
the specific data set. In this case, it can be assumed that if a driver
amount was not entered, it likely should have been zero; however,
in other instances, the intended value may not be as clear.

While this dataset isn't too complex, there are times when
we might need to remove some columns. To do this, we use the
.drop() method. The .drop() method takes in many optional
arguments, but we will only worry about "columns", the columns
we want to drop, and "inplace", if we want to modify in place or
not. Columns can be a single column name, or a list of column
names.

If we were not interested in the gender of drivers, we could drop that from our DataFrame. When making large changes to a DataFrame, it is better not to modify the original in place, but to assign the changed DataFrame to a new variable in case we want to refer back to the original data.

Commands

```python
import pandas as pd
df = pd.read_csv(
    "Licensed_Drivers__by_state__gender__and_age_group.csv"
    )
pd.set_option('display.float_format', '{:.2f}'.format)
df = df.fillna(0)

newdf = df.drop(columns = "Gender")
print(newdf.head())
```

Output

```
   Year   Cohort      State      Drivers
0  2017  Under 16    Alabama        0.00
1  2017  Under 16     Alaska        0.00
2  2017  Under 16    Arizona        0.00
3  2017  Under 16   Arkansas        0.00
4  2017  Under 16  California       0.00
```

Another useful technique is filtering data. In this case we have multiple years' worth of data, but maybe we are only interested in the most recent, in this case 2018. Once we have filtered our list we can also drop the year data.

Filtering a list can look a little confusing. First we create an array of True and False values based on the condition that we want to filter by, then we pass that in as a filter to generate a new DataFrame which we will store under another variable. This is typically done in one line, but for illustration it is split up here:

Truth array where the column "Year" equals 2018	```print(df ["Year"] == 2018)```	```0 False 1 False 2 False 3 False 4 False ... 57829 True 57830 True 57831 True 57832 True 57833 True Name: Year, Length: 57834, dtype: bool```
New DataFrame where the "Year" column equals 2018	```recent = (df[df ["Year"] == 2018]) print (recent)```	``` Year Gender Cohort State Drivers 55488 2018 Male Under16 Alabama 0.00 55489 2018 Male 16 Alabama 23176.00 55490 2018 Male 17 Alabama 26675.00 55491 2018 Male 18 Alabama 29728.00 55492 2018 Male 19 Alabama 30551.00 ... ... 57829 2018 Female 65-69 Wyoming 16061.00 57830 2018 Female 70-74 Wyoming 11804.00 57831 2018 Female 75-79 Wyoming 7770.00 57832 2018 Female 80-84 Wyoming 4715.00 57833 2018 Female 85+ Wyoming 3456.00 [2346 rows x 5 columns]```

So how does this help with business? Imagine we wanted to target young drivers in the United States, but we had a limited advertising budget. We could get a DataFrame with just the drivers under 16 per state with just a few lines of code.

Commands

```
import pandas as pd
df = pd.read_csv(
    "Licensed_Drivers__by_state__gender__and_age_group.csv"
    )
pd.set_option('display.float_format', '{:.2f}'.format)
df = df.fillna(0)
newdf = df.drop(columns = "Gender")
print(newdf.head())
```

Output

```
       Cohort     State         Drivers
55488  Under 16   Alabama       0.00
55511  Under 16   Alabama       0.00
55534  Under 16   Alaska        0.00
55557  Under 16   Alaska        0.00
55580  Under 16   Arizona       0.00
```

This is why previewing our data with `.head()` is so important. We can see here that our data is duplicated, since we had both male and female data. We can solve this issue by using `.groupby()`. This method is a little intense in terms of its *syntax*, but it is extremely useful. In general, we write it in the format of:

```
df.groupby(column_to_group_by)[column_to_
combine].function_that_combines
```

In this case, we want to group the states together and combine the drivers together by summing them, so we use:

```
young_drivers = young_drivers.groupby("State")
["Drivers"].sum()
```

Other common ways of combining values, also known as aggregating, are `.mean()`, `.count()`, `.min()`, and `.max()`.

We will also want to be able to sort our data and we use the aptly named `sort_values()` method to do so. By default, `.sort_values()` sorts from lowest to highest, so if we want the opposite we need to pass in the optional argument ascending as

False. Now we can see which states have the most drivers under 16 and target advertising to the youth in those states.

Commands

```
import pandas as pd
df = pd.read_csv(
    "Licensed_Drivers__by_state__gender__and_age_group.csv"
    )
pd.set_option('display.float_format', '{:.2f}'.format)
df.fillna(0, inplace = True)

recent = df[df["Year"] == 2018]
recent = recent.drop(columns = ["Year","Gender"])

young_drivers = recent[recent["Cohort"] == "Under 16"]
young_drivers = (
    young_drivers.groupby("State")["Drivers"].sum()
    )
y_drivers = young_drivers.sort_values(ascending=False)

print(y_drivers.head())
```

Output

```
State
South Carolina    27327.00
Kansas             8990.00
North Dakota       3371.00
Idaho              3309.00
Alabama               0.00
Name: Drivers, dtype: float64
```

Technically we have now reduced our DataFrame into a Series with just our states as the indices and the total drives as the values. Reducing our data down like this simplifies the analysis and as we see in the next section, makes it easier to display nice graphs and charts.

This is just a limited sense of what we can accomplish with just this one dataset. We could compare trends over time, look at gender-based data, or even group states based on geographical data. The steps taken here in terms of loading the data, filling or deleting null data, dropping information and filtering data, and finally aggregating and sorting data to draw conclusions are at the heart of all data analysis.

7.3 Leveraging Python for Business Insights

7.3.1 Setting up Matplotlib

It is cliché, but a picture really is worth a thousand words. We looked at how we can take complex datasets and gain valuable insights from them, but having the ability to create charts to represent our findings makes communications of these insights much more impressive. Since we are familiar with our licensing dataset, we will continue to use it in this section.

To create our visuals, we will use Matplotlib. Since the name is a bit tricky and involves a lot of characters, we will be shortening it as we did with Pandas. Matplotlib has many applications, but we will focus on using it to create graphs such as line charts, bar charts, histograms, scatter plots, and more. We will also leverage Pandas to simplify the process of creating graphs, although Matplotlib can be used with various types of data as well.

First, we have to make sure Matplotlib is installed, so we again run "pip install matplotlib" or handle it through our online IDE. The pyplot module of Matplotlib comes with many useful functions that we can use to make aesthetically pleasing graphs with little effort. When we import this library, we are only interested in the pyplot module of Matplotlib, so we "import matplotlib.pyplot as plt". which makes referencing its functions more convenient. Table 7.4 shows some functions which we can use, but there are many more to explore, along with additional functionalities. For more information, check the Matplotlib documentation.[21]

---

21. Matplotlib, "Matplotlib documentation – Matplotlib 3.9.0 documentation", accessed July 3, 2024, https://matplotlib.org/stable/

Table 7.4	Useful matplotlib.pyplot functions
`figure()`	The container for the graph. Takes an optional figsize argument which is a tuple that sets the size of the figure.
`title()`	The title of the graph, passed as a string.
`xlabel()`	The label on the x-axis, passed as a string.
`ylabel()`	The label on the y-axis, passed as a string.
`xticks()`	Used for fine tuning the ticks on the x-axis. Optional rotation argument can be used to set the angle of the labels in degrees.
`yticks()`	Used for fine tuning the ticks on the y-axis. Optional rotation argument can be used to set the angle of the labels in degrees.
`grid()`	Pass True to show the grid. There are additional options as well.
`tight_layout()`	Used to remove padding around the figure. Best when there is a lot of information to fit.
`show()`	Display the graph, otherwise we can't see it. The code pauses while the graph is being displayed.

We do not always need to use all of these and if we're not particular we can create graphs just using .figure() and .show() but a little extra effort makes the overall appearance much nicer. To create the actual graphs, we will use the .plot() method of Pandas DataFrames since that is how our data is already stored. Matplotlib could handle this on its own, but since we already have the data in the correct format, it just makes sense.

The plot method takes a number of optional arguments, but for us the most important is "kind" which determines which type of graph to draw, such as line, bar, pie, histogram, among others.[22]

---

22. Pandas, "pandas.DataFrame.plot – pandas 2.2.2 documentation", accessed July 3, 2024, https://pandas.pydata.org/docs/reference/api/pandas.DataFrame.plot.html

7.3.2 Line Graphs

A line graph can be used to show trends over time, a very valuable insight to have in business. A line graph displays data points connected by straight lines on a regular grid. Typically, a value such as cost or amount would be graphed against time.

If we wanted to draw a line graph of the number of drivers in California over time, we would load in our data as before, filter our data to include only California, and then group the driver information by summing it together, based on the year.

```python
import pandas as pd
import matplotlib.pyplot as plt
df = pd.read_csv(
    "Licensed_Drivers__by_state__gender__and_age_group.csv"
    )
state_data = df[df["State"] == "California"]
year_data = state_data.groupby("Year")["Drivers"].sum()
plt.figure()
year_data.plot(
    kind='line',marker='o',linestyle='solid',color='b'
    )
plt.title('Total Drivers in California Over Time')
plt.ylabel('Number of Drivers')
plt.grid(True)
plt.show()
```

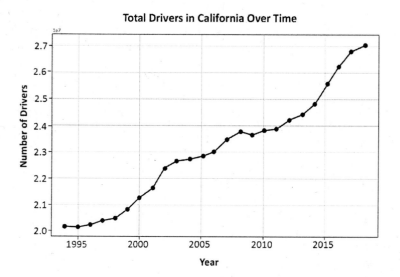

Total Drivers in California Over Time

We can clearly see here that the number of drivers in California is steadily increasing.

A few interesting things to note. We didn't need to set the x-axis label, since the data already had the label "Year", but we did set the y-axis, since it would have defaulted to the label in the data "Drivers". This would be fine, but "Number of Drivers" seems a little more appropriate. To better read the graph, we included a grid as well, but this was optional. There are also some optional arguments to set the marker style, line style, and color here, but other than that it should be very straightforward. Table 7.5 shows some options for these arguments, but it would be a great idea to consult the Matplotlib documentation for more options.[23]

---

23. Matplotlib, "matplotlib.markers – Matplotlib 3.9.0 documentation", accessed July 3, 2024,
https://matplotlib.org/stable/api/markers_api.html#module-matplotlib.markers

Matplotlib, "matplotlib.lines.Line2D – Matplotlib 3.9.0 documentation", accessed July 3, 2024
https://matplotlib.org/stable/api/_as_gen/matplotlib.lines.Line2D.html#matplotlib.lines.Line2D.set_linestyle

Matplotlib, "Specifying colors – Matplotlib 3.9.0 documentation", accessed July 3, 2024, https://matplotlib.org/stable/users/explain/colors/colors.html#sphx-glr-users-explain-colors-colors-py

Table 7.5	Common options for modifying graphs in Matplotlib
Marker	
"o"	Circle
"x"	X-shape
"s"	square
Linestyle	
"solid"	A solid line
"dashed"	A dashed line
"dotted"	A dotted line
Color	
"b"	Blue lines
"g"	Green lines
"r"	Red lines

In this DataFrame, we were only left with two columns, which were understood by Matplotlib and Pandas as x and y axis data, however there are times where our DataFrames may not be so organized. We can specify the x and y data by passing them as optional arguments in our plot statement `df.plot(kind='line', x = 'x_information', y = 'y_information')`.

For example, if we have the following CSV, there are multiple columns so we would need to specify our *x* and *y*.

```
Date,Sales,Expenses
2023-01-01,100,50
2023-01-02,150,60
2023-01-03,130,55
2023-01-04,170,70
2023-01-05,160,65
2023-01-06,180,80
2023-01-07,190,85
```

If we try to graph this DataFrame without specifying the x and y data, we get something like Figure 7.3. This is because the default index is used for the x-axis, which just labels the points from 0 to 6. By default, all of the numerical data is graphed as individual Series against this default index.

Figure 7.3 **Sales and Expenses vs Index, df.plot(kind='line')**

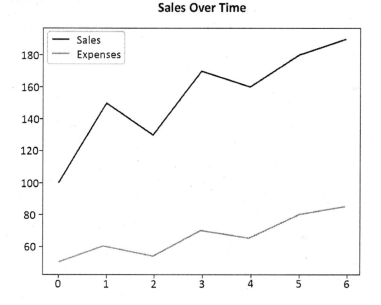

To only graph the sales data against the date, we instead use the optional x and y arguments indicating the appropriate columns, as seen in Figure 7.4.

Figure 7.4 **Sales vs Date, df.plot(kind='line', x='Date', y='Sales')**

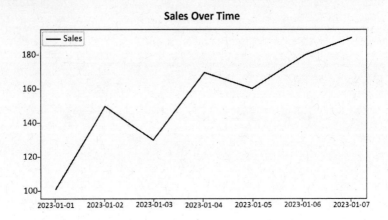

7.3.3 Pie Charts

Pie charts can be used to illustrate the proportions between categories of items. In business, this is great for looking at demographics of customers or income sources. Pie charts work best when we are not concerned with exact values but want a quick comparison between a small number of categories.

If we wanted to compare the number of male and female drivers in 2018, we would go through our data process as normal and group our drivers by gender, summing them up. Creating the plot is the same as with line graphs, but we need to use "kind='pie'". Optionally we can specify the colors that we want used in a list. These colors are repeated if we have more categories than colors, and Matplotlib will supply default colors if we do not specify them. If we wish to display the percentage, we use the optional argument "autopct='%1.1f%%'". There are other ways to add the percentage, but this is the common method. We've seen this formatting before, but since the formatting is consistently used in this way, we won't worry about the details.

We don't need to supply the x-axis as the labels in the data are appropriate for the graph. We use `plt.ylabel('')` to display a blank label on the y-axis. It also doesn't make sense to add in a grid, so we don't include that statement.

```python
import pandas as pd
import matplotlib.pyplot as plt

df = pd.read_csv(
    "Licensed_Drivers__by_state__gender__and_age_group.csv"
    )
data_2018 = df[df["Year"] == 2018]
gender_data = data_2018.groupby("Gender")["Drivers"].sum()

plt.figure()
gender_data.plot(
    kind='pie', autopct='%1.1f%%', colors=['r','b']
    )
plt.title('Male vs Female Drivers in 2018')
plt.ylabel('')
plt.show()
```

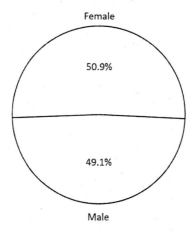

Male vs Female Drivers in 2018

Female

50.9%

49.1%

Male

Here we can quickly see that while there are more female drivers than male drivers however the percentage is very close, and would not be statistically significant.

Much like the previous example, in this DataFrame, we were only left with two columns, so we don't need to specify the columns to use for the data. If we want to be specific about the columns, we can specify the y information the same as with our line graph, but the pie graph expects labels, not x data. We can use the optional argument "labels" to handle this situation. We can pass either a list of data, or since we already have the information in a DataFrame, we can access it as `df['label_data']`.

We can specify the x and y data by passing them as optional arguments in our plot statement `df.plot(kind='pie', y = 'y_information', label = df['label_data'])`.

For example, this CSV data would produce a DataFrame with multiple columns.

```
Item,Stock,Warehouse
Laptops,120,North
Smartphones,80,South
Tablets,50,East
Headphones,30,West
Monitors,70,North
Keyboards,40,South
Mice,60,East
Printers,90,West
```

To properly display the pie chart of the stock we can directly use the statement "df.plot(kind='pie', y='Stock', labels=df['Item'], autopct='%1.1f%%')" to generate the chart as seen in Figure 7.5.

Figure 7.5   **Specifying y and label values**

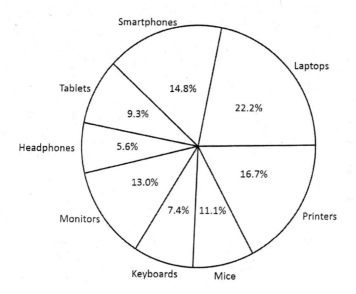

7.3.4 Bar Graphs

A bar graph displays data using rectangular bars with their size proportional to the values they represent. It is similar to a pie chart; however, it can be easier to display more information and compare many categories. There are also special bar graphs called histograms which show the distribution of a dataset based on bins of information. These are often a range of values, and when used this way can be used to find patterns and outliers in data, but we won't go into details of them here.

Here we will use a bar graph to display the number of drivers in each state. As before, we load our data and group by state, summing up the drivers. This is very similar to our other examples, but there are two notable pieces. First, our states are the labels on our bars, but writing them horizontally will take up too much room, so we can set the rotation of the ticks on the x-axis by using the statement "plt.xticks(rotation=90)". We will also use a tight outline, `plt.tight_layout()`, in order to maximize the space by removing some of the padding. This is necessary as there are many states to display.

```python
import pandas as pd
import matplotlib.pyplot as plt
df = pd.read_csv(
    "Licensed_Drivers__by_state__gender__and_age_group.csv"
    )
data_2018 = df[df["Year"] == 2018]
state_drivers_2018 = (
    data_2018.groupby("State")["Drivers"].sum()
    )
plt.figure()
state_drivers_2018.plot(kind='bar', color='g')
plt.title('Total Drivers per State in 2018')
plt.ylabel('Number of Drivers')
plt.xticks(rotation=90)
plt.tight_layout()
plt.show()
```

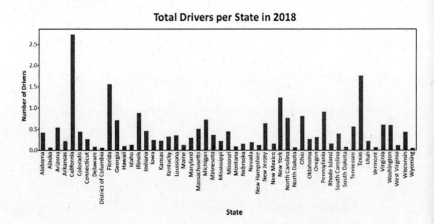

This allows us to quickly see that the greatest number of drivers by far are in California, but Florida and Texas also have large amounts of drivers. This could help us with targeting our advertising strategies.

You can specify x and y data in the same way as with line graphs, if needed.

7.4 Advancing Your Career with Python Skills

One of the key takeaways from this chapter is that data analysis is extremely important for businesses to grow and succeed. Having people outside of a business analyze data can be effective, but it is much better to have someone who knows the business analyze the data, as they would have insight as to what to look for. By understanding and interpreting complex datasets, we can identify strategies to improve our business models. Whether we work in finance, marketing, healthcare, or another industry, our proficiency with programming and data analysis can make us valuable assets.

Spreadsheets are widely used in business to analyze data, and while they have their uses, Python offers several advantages over traditional spreadsheets.

- **Scalability:** Using traditional spreadsheets becomes much more difficult when working with large datasets. Using the Pandas library, we can handle many datasets which would be impossible with a spreadsheet.

- **Automation:** When our data changes, we can simply rerun our Python script to produce new results. As long as the headings of our data remain the same, our programs should produce usable results. Compare this to a spreadsheet where we would have to add in our formulas and set up our graphs with each new version of the data.

- **Advanced Analytics:** While only briefly mentioned in this chapter, we can apply machine learning to our datasets in Python and get the benefit of using AI to find more complex relationships within our data and make predictions from it.

- **Integration:** Python can also load many different types of data from many different sources. Web scraping, which we will discuss in Chapter 9, takes data from websites. APIs allow us to draw information directly from web services, giving us more up-to-date information. Spreadsheets are much more static in nature.

As Python programmers, we bring a lot of skills to the table when it comes to data analysis and this chapter really just scratches the surface. As we have discussed, this goes beyond purely technical roles. Our ability to solve problems and analyze data can give us a competitive edge in almost any industry. Combining this with our skills in data visualization, and Python in general, can make us valuable to potential employers.

Quiz

1. **What is the first step in data analysis?**
   a. Data analysis
   b. Data cleaning
   c. Data collection
   d. Data visualization

2. **What is the main purpose of data analytics in business?**
   a. To automate all business processes
   b. To drive insights and inform decisions
   c. To replace decisions made by people
   d. To maintain data privacy

3. **A programmer has a large dataset that they want to clean and analyze. Which library will be the most helpful to them?**
   a. CSV
   b. Math
   c. Matplotlib
   d. Pandas

4. **Which function is used to read a CSV file?**
   a. `pd.read_csv()`
   b. `pd.load_csv()`
   c. `pd.open_csv()`
   d. `pd.import_csv()`

5. **Which method previews the beginning rows of a DataFrame, df?**

   a. `df.describe()`

   b. `df.head()`

   c. `df.info()`

   d. `df.top()`

6. **Which file format stores information in this way?**

   ```
   ID,Name,Age,Salary,Department
   1,John,30,70000,Engineering
   2,Emily,40,90000,HR
   3,Michael,25,50000,Sales
   4,Sarah,35,85000,Finance
   5,David,28,62000,IT
   ```

   a. CSV

   b. JSON

   c. SQL

   d. XML

7. **A DataFrame, df, has lots of missing values. Which method will help clean the data?**

   a. `df.clean()`

   b. `df.dropna()`

   c. `df.tail()`

   d. `df.removena()`

8. What tasks does the following code perform?

```
import pandas as pd
df = pd.read_csv('sales_data.csv')
print(df.describe())
```

a. Reads a CSV and performs basic statistics on it

b. Reads a CSV and prints the last five rows

c. Writes a CSV with the summary of the data

d. Writes a CSV with the statistical analysis of a dataset

9. Why is it important to clean data?

a. To create visualizations

b. To enhance the data in the set

c. To ensure the data is accurate and reliable

d. To ensure there are no viruses present

10. What is the purpose of the `.describe()` method of DataFrames?

a. To clean the data

b. To display statistics about the data

c. To preview the data

d. To see the types of data

Answers	1 – b	2 – b	3 – d	4 – a	5 – b
	6 – a	7 – b	8 – a	9 – c	10 – b

Chapter Summary

◆ Data is extremely useful to provide business insights.

◆ CSV files are an easy and effective way to store and retrieve data.

◆ Pandas can be used to load, clean, and manipulate data.

◆ Matplotlib works well with Pandas to create data visualizations.

◆ Data analytics skills can significantly enhance employability.

Chapter 8

Case Studies

In this chapter we take a different approach. Instead of learning new topics, we will apply our skills to solving case studies that mimic real-world situations. While concepts like syntax, object-oriented programming, and error handling are important, being able to tie them all together to create a program that solves a problem is a much more important skill. In many ways, this chapter serves as a culmination of all the previous chapters

The key learning objectives of this chapter are:

- Understanding how to approach real-world applications

- Exploring how to use different techniques to approach problems

- Gaining experience in working with datasets

8.1 Introduction

Real-world applications are crucial for reinforcing the concepts we have covered in the previous chapters. After all, we will likely use our Python programming skills to write applications to solve real-world problems. The best way to learn programming is by actually doing it.

While there will be hints and tips, as well as detailed solutions to the problems in the case studies, it is recommended that you attempt them first. Hands-on practice and problem-solving can help programmers gain confidence and gain a deeper understanding of Python syntax.

Before trying to tackle any of these problems, it is important to make sure we understand the requirements. Re-read the question and ensure everything is fully understood. This ensures that we are focused on creating an effective solution with the objectives of the problem in mind. Otherwise, we might waste time focusing on the less important parts of a problem. These problems will be given with *constraints*. Constraints help us further focus on what is important. This guides us towards an optimal solution as they will often give some practical limits to the problem at hand. They can also prevent us from missing some critical information that we could otherwise overlook.

Similar in nature are *edge cases*. Edge cases are the rare and often unexpected situations that occur that could cause trouble if we do not consider them. This could be when a user enters the wrong type of data, or a value falls right on the edge of a category. Edge cases are not specifically written out with these case studies, but they are important to consider as they ensure our programs function for all conditions, regardless of how extreme they could be. This makes our programs more resilient and dependable.

When approaching these problems, it is a good idea to start with a pen and paper. How could the task be completed without technology? Start with a flowchart or pseudocode to get ideas down. Look back over previous chapters to remind yourself of some of the techniques that may help. Don't be discouraged if you have to look at the potential solutions before creating your own unique solutions.

8.2 Case Study 1: Change Calculation System

Description

Beckett is a supervisor at QuickMart, a fictional retail store. He noticed that some of his employees struggle to quickly determine the optimal way to return change. He would like to have a system that given the total count and the money provided by the customer, will calculate the correct change using the proper denominations.

Constraints

Change can be given in $50, $20, $10, $5, $1, 0.25¢, 0.10¢, 0.05¢, and 0.01¢ denominations.

Task

Write a Python program that calculates the correct change. The total amount due and the total amount of money received will both be entered by the user.

Hints

Use a dictionary to store the count of each denomination. It may be easier to convert your values to cents to avoid issues with floating points. Be sure to check if the cash given is enough to cover the total amount due.

Potential Solution

This problem is easier to approach if we break it down into parts. First, we will need to handle the input and ensure the correct amount of cash is given. Second, we need to figure out the amount of money to be returned, and the proper amounts of each denomination to return. Finally, we need to report the amounts to be returned in some useful format. In order to make things easier, we can use three functions and a main program.

The main program will take the user input and then determine if there is enough money provided to make the purchase at all. If so, it will call the other three functions, which we will name "calculate_change", "determine_denominations", and "display_change".

```
total_due = float(input("Enter the total amount due: "))
cash_given = float(input("Enter the cash given: "))
if cash_given < total_due:
  print("Error: Cash given is less than the total due.")
else:
  change = calculate_change(total_due, cash_given)
  denominations = determine_denominations(change)
  display_change(denominations)
```

The "calculate_change" function will simply return the difference between the total given and the total due. This does not seem like it needs to be its own function, but keeping it separate from the main program allows us to make changes to it without affecting the rest of the program. This could be helpful later if we wanted to add tipping options or rounding for donations.

```
def calculate_change(total_due, cash_given):
    return cash_given - total_due
```

The main component of this problem would be determining the denominations of change to return. Depending on your approach, there can be many ways to handle this. The main idea here is to loop over each of the denominations from highest to lowest and see how many of each evenly divides in. For example, if the change due is $28.35, no $50s will be returned, but there is a $20 that can be returned, leaving $8.35. We would then proceed with $10s, $5s, and so on. In order to handle the names and the value of the currency, we will use a dictionary to store the names as keys and the value, in cents, as values.

```
denominations = {
    '$50': 5000, '$20': 2000, '$10': 1000,
    '$5': 500, '$1': 100, '25¢': 25,
    '10¢': 10, '5¢': 5, '1¢':1
}
```

We will work in cents for two reasons. First, it avoids some of the issues with floating point values rounding. Second, we can use the modulus operator, %, to find out how much change is left to give back. We will store the results in a second dictionary which will also have the name as the key and the value will be the amount of the denomination to be returned.

```
def determine_denominations(change):
  denominations = {
    '$50': 5000, '$20': 2000, '$10': 1000,
    '$5': 500, '$1': 100, '25¢': 25,
    '10¢': 10, '5¢': 5, '1¢':1
    }
  correct_change = {}
  change = int(round(change * 100))

  for value, cents in denominations.items():
    amount = int(change / cents)
    if amount > 0:
      correct_change[value] = amount
      change = change % cents
    return correct_change
```

By inserting the *key-value pairs* as we create them, we will have no record of denominations that we do not need, and therefore will not need any logic to skip over denominations with a value of 0.

Finally, we display the amounts of each denomination to be returned to the customer. In our "display_change" function, we pass in the returned dictionary and loop through it once more, using `items()` to get both the key and the value. First, we check if the count is greater than zero, and if it is, we print it.

```
def display_change(denominations):
  print("Change to be given:")
  for value, count in denominations.items():
    if count > 0:
      print(f"{count} x {value}")
```

Sample Input
```
Enter the total amount due: 124.99
Enter the cash given: 150
```

Output
```
Change to be given:
1 x $20
1 x $5
1 x 1¢
```

Again, there are multiple ways to approach this problem and this is only one potential solution.

8.3 Case Study 2: Optimizing Employee Scheduling for a Small Business

Description

You are the manager at a small retail store with three employees: Sam, Jack, and Emmalena. You need to create a weekly schedule that ensures at least one employee is working each day from Monday to Friday, from 9 am to 5 pm.

Constraints

Sam is available on Monday, Tuesday, and Wednesday and can work up to 20 hours per week. Jack is available on Tuesday, Thursday, and Friday, and can work up to 15 hours per week. Emmalena is available on Monday, Wednesday, and Friday, and can work up to 25 hours per week. Each shift is 8 hours long.

Task

Write a Python program to create a schedule that assigns employees to shifts based on their availability and ensure they do not exceed their maximum working hours.

Hints

This task can be done in multiple ways, but taking an *object-oriented* approach may help keep the employee logic separate from the rest of the code and avoid the use of complex dictionaries. Instances of *classes* can be stored in *lists* like any other data type. *Loops* and *conditionals* can be used to assign employees to shifts. Be sure to keep track of the hours each employee is scheduled to ensure they do not exceed their limits.

There are also some useful libraries that could help with this task. It would be a good idea to use the shuffle() function that is part of the random library. If you pass a list to it, it randomizes the order in place. This could be useful if the first schedule attempt is unsuccessful.

Potential Solution

We will definitely want an "Employee" class that holds the employee's name, availability, maximum hours, and scheduled hours. There should be a method for determining an employee's availability on a particular day as well. Once instances of our Employee class are created (one per employee) we can store them in a list for efficient looping. Navigating through the week may be tricky, but we'll start with a dictionary to add employees as the shifts are filled.

While not strictly necessary, it would be nice to have two functions, one for assigning the shifts and one for displaying the work schedule. This is also a situation where we may not find a possible solution, so we should consider how we would address that as well.

Our main block of code is fairly simple here. At the top, we need to import the shuffle() function from the random library. This is so we can try a different combination of employees if we do not have an employee assigned to every day. In a real sense, we also would want to vary the schedule so that our employees do not always have the same shifts. Who wants to work every Friday if they can avoid it?

Next, we will need to create instances of each of our employees. We will need to pass in the employee's name, availability, and maximum hours. Once created, we will add them into a list. This list will get passed into our make_schedule function which will return the schedule or "None" if the schedule fails to be created.

If no schedule is created, there should be some output for this. Otherwise, we should pass the schedule into our show_ schedule function. This may not need to be its own function, but organizing it this way makes it easier for us so we can make changes without affecting the rest of the program.

```
from random import shuffle

#Employee class code
#make_schedule code
#show_schedule code

sam = Employee(
  "Sam", ["Monday","Tuesday","Wednesday"],20
  )
jack = Employee(
  "Jack", ["Tuesday","Thursday","Friday"],15
  )
emmalena = Employee(
  "Emmalena",["Monday","Wednesday","Friday"], 25
  )
employees = [sam,jack,emmalena]
schedule = make_schedule(employees)
if not schedule:
  print("error making schedule, hire more employees?")
else:
  show_schedule(schedule)
```

In this situation, we only need a single class for the employees, with a *constructor* to set the initial values, an `is_available` method that takes in the day and returns True or False, an `assign_shift` method which assigns the day, and increases their hours, and a `reset_schedule` method in case we need to restart the schedule.

```python
class Employee:
  def __init__(self, name, availability, max_hours):
    self.name = name
    self.__availability = availability
    self.__max_hours = max_hours
    self.__current_hours = 0
    self.schedule = []
  def is_available(self, day):
    if self.__current_hours + 8 > self.__max_hours:
      return False
    elif day in self.__availability:
      return True
    else:
      return False
  def assign_shift(self, day):
    self.schedule.append(day)
    self.__current_hours += 8
  def reset_schedule(self):
    self.__current_hours = 0
    self.schedule = []
```

In our Employee class, the name and schedule are *public* for ease of access, but all other *attributes* are *private* to prevent accidental changes. The `is_available` method first checks to see if eight more hours would put an employee over the allowed hours then checks if they are available. Handling this inside the class makes it easier to adjust later. The `assign_shift` simply adds the day to their individual schedule and increases their hours. Since there is a chance that we do not correctly create a schedule to meet all of the requirements, the `reset_schedule` method sets `current_hours` back to 0 and makes the "schedule" an empty list so we can try again.

If we weren't worried about the potential failure of the schedule being created, the make_schedule function would be a little simpler, but the logic shouldn't be too hard to follow. First, we set up two *variables* to determine if we are done looping. valid_schedule is set to False at the beginning of the function and is updated to True once a valid schedule is created. "attempts" is set to 0 and increased by 1 each time there is a failure. This way we can avoid the potential infinite loop if there is no possible correct schedule.

We will use a while-loop as we do not know how many loops it will take. We will loop while the schedule is not valid and the attempts are less than 1000. This may seem like a lot, and with only three employees we won't need that many attempts, but Python can handle 1000 loops in almost no time so it's a pretty safe number.

We use a dictionary to hold the days of the week and who is working, starting with "None" at first since no one is assigned. Next, we loop over the keys, which are the days of the week, and loop through the employees until we find one who is available. Once we find an available employee, we assign them to the day and update their information before breaking out of the loop for that day.

Once we have gone through the week, we check to make sure none of the values() are still "None" If there is a "None" value, we reset, add one to our attempts, reshuffle the employee list, and try again. Once we find a valid schedule we return it. If we do not find a valid schedule we return "None".

```
def make_schedule(employees):

valid_schedule = False
  attempts = 0

  while not valid_schedule and attempts < 1000:
    shuffle(employees)

    schedule = {
      "Monday":None, "Tuesday":None, "Wednesday": None,
      "Thursday":None, "Friday":None
      }

    for day in schedule.keys():
      for employee in employees:
        if employee.is_available(day):
          employee.assign_shift(day)
          schedule[day] = employee.name
          break

    if not None in schedule.values():
      valid_schedule = True
      return schedule
    else:
      attempts += 1
      for employee in employees:
        employee.reset_schedule()
  return None
```

Finally, to show the schedule we loop through the items in our schedule dictionary and print them out nicely.

```
def show_schedule(schedule):
  for day, employee in schedule.items():
    print(f'{day} --> {employee}')
```

This exercise highlights the power of using classes to separate and organize your code. Solving this problem without using object-oriented programming would be much less streamlined and would involve rather complex dictionaries of information. The random shuffling of the employee list may not be the most efficient method since we may produce the same list several times while searching for a valid schedule. The itertools library has many functions that could make this task more streamlined. The documentation can be found at https://docs.python.org/3/library/itertools.html.

8.4 Case Study 3: Data Analysis to Find an Investment Opportunity

Description

Sophie wants to invest in real estate property in Maryland and has obtained a CSV of the sales by zip code from 2010 – 2022, available at https://catalog.data.gov/dataset/maryland-total-residential-sales-2010-2022-zip-codes. The dataset is too complicated to analyze by hand, so she would like a Python program that can be used to determine which jurisdiction has increasing sales and then to compare the total sales in 2022 in those jurisdictions depending on zip code to help her decide where to invest.

Constraints

As per usual, the data needs to be verified and cleaned. Bar graphs should be used to determine the trends in each jurisdiction. Another bar graph should be used to visualize the sales in the individual zip codes.

Task

Write a Python program that uses Pandas and Matplotlib to clean and visualize residential sales data in Maryland in order to determine the best area to invest in.

Hints

The data needs to be verified, so using the `info()` method would be a great start. Review how to filter and group data from Chapter 7. It would be a good idea to make new DataFrames instead of overwriting the original DataFrame as you make changes.

Potential Solution

This dataset may be updated as more information is collected, so the particular details in the explanation may be different if the code is run in the future.

Working with data tends to be a more "code as you go" situation, but that doesn't mean we can't strategize our method. First, we will need to import our libraries, load our data, and ensure there is no missing information.

```
import pandas as pd
import matplotlib.pyplot as plt

sales_data = pd.read_csv("Maryland_Total_Residential_
Sales_2010_-_2022_Zip_Codes.csv")
sales_data.info()

print('\namount of null data')
print(sales_data.isnull().sum())
```

Output

```
<class 'pandas.core.frame.DataFrame'>
RangeIndex: 526 entries, 0 to 525
Data columns (total 15 columns):
 #   Column                  Non-Null Count   Dtype
---  ------                  --------------   -----
 0   Data Created            526 non-null     object
 1   Jurisdiction            526 non-null     object
 2   Zip Code                526 non-null     int64
 3   2010 Residential Sales  526 n`on-null    int64
 4   2011 Residential Sales  526 non-null     int64
 5   2012 Residential Sales  526 non-null     int64
 6   2013 Residential Sales  526 non-null     int64
 7   2014 Residential Sales  526 non-null     int64
 8   2015 Residential Sales  526 non-null     int64
 9   2016 Residential Sales  526 non-null     int64
 10  2017 Residential Sales  526 non-null     int64
 11  2018 Residential Sales  526 non-null     int64
 12  2019 Residential Sales  526 non-null     int64
 13  2020 Residential Sales  526 non-null     int64
 14  2021 Residential Sales  526 non-null     int64
dtypes: int64(13), object(2)
memory usage: 61.8+ KB

amount of null data
Data Created            0
Jurisdiction            0
Zip Code                0
2010 Residential Sales  0
2011 Residential Sales  0
2012 Residential Sales  0
2013 Residential Sales  0
2014 Residential Sales  0
2015 Residential Sales  0
2016 Residential Sales  0
2017 Residential Sales  0
2018 Residential Sales  0
2019 Residential Sales  0
2020 Residential Sales  0
2021 Residential Sales  0
dtype: int64
```

We've got a lot of headings, but luckily no missing data. Since the "Data Created" heading is not needed we will drop that information. We will also filter out the older data and group the new data by jurisdiction. This will allow us to focus on the most recent information on jurisdiction first. We will need the zip code information later, so instead of overwriting the original data, we will save this as a new DataFrame.

```
sales_data = sales_data.drop(columns="Data Created")
jurisdiction_data = (
  sales_data.groupby("Jurisdiction")["2021 Residential
  Sales"].sum()
  )
print(jurisdiction_data.head())
```

Output

```
<class 'pandas.core.series.Series'>
Index: 24 entries, ALLEGANY to WORCESTER
Series name: 2021 Residential Sales
Non-Null Count  Dtype
--------------  -----
24 non-null     int64
dtypes: int64(1)
memory usage: 384.0+ bytes
Jurisdiction
ALLEGANY              856
ANNE ARUNDEL       12599
BALTIMORE          13943
BALTIMORE CITY         0
CALVERT             2171
Name: 2021 Residential Sales, dtype: int64
```

Previewing our data, we can see that we have reduced our dataset down significantly. We can easily display this information on a bar graph, however it would still be a little cramped for a pie chart.

```
plt.figure()
jurisdiction_data.plot(kind='bar')
plt.title("Sales in 2021 Based on Jurisdiction")
plt.tight_layout()
plt.show()
```

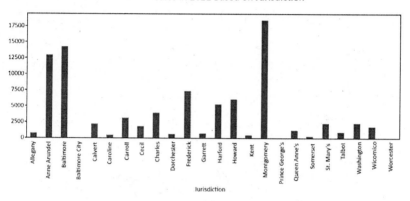

Now we can quickly see that Montgomery has the greatest sales, so we can focus on that area. We can filter out everything except the Montgomery data.

```
montgomery_data = (
    sales_data[sales_data["Jurisdiction"]== "MONTGOMERY"]
    )
print(montgomery_data.head())
```

Output

	Jurisdiction	Zip Code	...	2020 Residential Sales	2021 Residential Sales
296	MONTGOMERY	20707	...	0	6
297	MONTGOMERY	20777	...	0	0
298	MONTGOMERY	20812	...	4	9
299	MONTGOMERY	20814	...	360	516
300	MONTGOMERY	20815	...	348	519

```
[5 rows x 14 columns]
```

We are left with a lot of information still, and we have a pesky index column at the beginning which our graphs may try to use.

Rather than dropping columns, we can just specify which columns we want to use as our x and y values. Since we still have 14 zip codes, as shown by the 14 columns, we are still best off using a bar graph.

```
plt.figure()
montgomery_data.plot(
    kind='bar', x="Zip Code", y="2021 Residential Sales"
)
plt.title("Sales in 2021 In Montgomery")
plt.show()
```

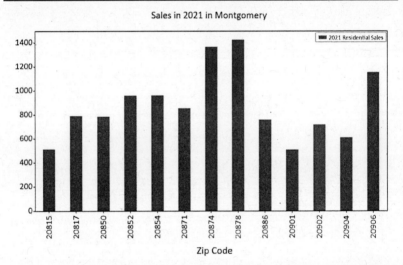

Now we can clearly see that the area indicated by the zip code 20878 has the most sales. Since 20874 is also close to the same sales, it is also worth investigating. We can recommend both to Sophie as possible investment opportunities.

8.5 Conclusion

These case studies each focused on different aspects of programming in Python and should have provided some insight into how to approach problems from different perspectives. If ten programmers were given these tasks, it is likely that we would get back ten different solutions, although there would be some similarities in them. There is no one right answer in programming and the act of problem solving should involve some creativity.

After writing a program to solve a problem, we, as programmers, are not actually finished. Our first approach to solving a problem may not be the most optimal one. As we become more proficient programmers, it is no longer good enough to have a problem that simply works. We want a program that works quickly with minimal memory usage. We won't focus on the details here as *algorithm complexity* is really not a beginner's topic, but the short version is that after we have finished writing a program, we should take another look and see if we can make it better, which usually means faster or more efficient.

We also need to review our code carefully to ensure that our code has no *errors*. At this point, it is important that we run extra tests to make sure the code is working fine for all cases. It is better to catch and fix bugs before we release a piece of software to anyone else to run.

Refactoring is another important step that early programmers tend to skip. Refactoring is about making our code more readable and aligning it to the current best practices. This is where we go back and see if we should break down complex sections into smaller pieces or replace redundant sections with a function that can be called instead. As beginners, we should start by making sure that the code we write isn't repeating itself.

If we get used to incorporating these ideas into our workflow, we will produce more optimal solutions and align ourselves with best practices in programming.

Quiz

1. **What is the purpose of using for loops in programming?**
   a. To create classes
   b. To define functions
   c. To handle errors
   d. To iterate over a sequence

2. **What is the purpose of the `def` keyword?**
   a. To define a class
   b. To define a function
   c. To define a loop
   d. To define a variable

3. **What is a function?**
   a. A block of code that runs when it is called
   b. A loop that iterates over a sequence
   c. A sequence of immutable characters
   d. A way to store multiple values and methods in a single variable

4. **When taking a modular programming approach, why are functions important?**
   a. To avoid using classes
   b. To create reusable, isolated pieces of code
   c. To ensure an appropriate code length
   d. To make code more impressive looking

5. **Which is not part of object-oriented programming?**

   a. Compilation

   b. Encapsulation

   c. Inheritance

   d. Polymorphism

6. **How are classes and functions different?**

   a. Classes allow for inheritance, but functions do not

   b. Classes are reusable, but functions are not

   c. Function define methods while classes define attributes

   d. Functions define behavior while classes do not

7. **Why is inheritance used in object-oriented programming?**

   a. To allow one class to share attributes and methods from another class

   b. To define multiple methods with the same name

   c. To hide the details of an object

   d. To store multiple values and methods in a single variable

8. **How can graphs and charts help in understanding data?**

   a. By avoiding the need for clean data

   b. By avoiding the need for complex analysis

   c. By removing null data points

   d. By providing a visual representation of patterns and trends

9. **What is the purpose of data cleaning?**

   a. To create charts and graphs

   b. To format data to print nicely

   c. To remove or fill in missing data in a dataset

   d. To store data in a database

10. **What is the best approach to learning programming?**

   a. Attending programming boot camps

   b. Programming itself

   c. Reading programming books

   d. Watching programming tutorials

Answers	1 – d	2 – b	3 – a	4 – b	5 – a
	6 – a	7 – a	8 – d	9 – c	10 – b

Chapter Summary

◆ Programming is not just about understanding syntax.

◆ Problem-solving is an important part of programming.

◆ After programs are written, reviewing and refactoring are important tasks

This page is intentionally left blank

Chapter **9**

Exploring Emerging Trends in Programming

In this chapter, we explore advanced topics that are emerging in programming today. We will be looking into the concepts more than the programming side of things. These topics are not specifically rooted in Python; however, Python's ease of use and extensive libraries make it an ideal choice for working with currently emerging trends. We will focus less on programming and more on the concepts. Learning to program in Python is not a straight path, but rather a journey across numerous pathways. In this chapter, we will explore some of these pathways. Whether it is machine learning, web design, interfacing with real-world devices, or scraping data from the internet, Python offers something for all developers.

The key learning objectives of this chapter are:

- Understanding the fundamental concepts of Artificial Intelligence and Machine Learning

- Understanding how Python can interface with real-world devices

- Understanding the principles of web scraping

- Understanding how frameworks like Flask and Django can create dynamic websites

- Understanding the role of cloud computing in modern applications

9.1 Exploring Artificial Intelligence and Machine Learning

Artificial Intelligence (AI) and Machine Learning (ML) are currently at the forefront of the industry. Public interest in AI has grown since OpenAI introduced ChatGPT to the public in late 2022.[24] While AI has been used in many industries and is certainly not a new concept, it has recently gained significant public attention. However, many people still do not have a clear understanding as to what AI and ML are, or how they are different from each other.

The exact definition of artificial intelligence is difficult to pin down, as it involves, reasoning, planning, learning, communicating, and perceiving information to make decisions.

24. OpenAI, "Introducing ChatGPT | OpenAI", published November 30, 2022, https://openai.com/index/chatgpt/

It also crosses boundaries as it becomes integrated into the software we interact with, becoming bundled with services.[25] At its heart, artificial intelligence uses technology to mimic human intelligence. Machine learning is a subset of artificial intelligence and involves the development of algorithms that allow computers to take a large amount of data and use it to make predictions. There is a lot of talk about using neural networks these days to analyze even more complex data. We call this deep learning, and it is a specialized branch of ML.

Figure 9.1   AI Hierarchy

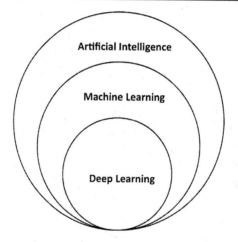

source: Image by Lollixzc, published August 19, 2022, Wikimedia Commons, https://commons.wikimedia.org/wiki/File:AI_hierarchy.svg

To understand the basics of AI, there are some key concepts to consider. First of all, we can break machine learning into two basic categories: *supervised learning* and *unsupervised learning*.

---

25. Samoili, Sofia, Marta Lopez Cobo, Boban Delipetrev, Francesca Martinez-Plumed, Eduardo Gomez Gutierrez, and Giuditta De Prato. AI Watch. Defining Artificial Intelligence 2.0. EUR 30873 EN. Luxembourg: Publications Office of the European Union, 2021. ISBN 978-92-76-42648-6. doi:10.2760/019901. JRC126426

Supervised learning involves giving an algorithm a set of labeled data. How many different types of data and how it is labeled depends on the application. For example, we may have hundreds of photos labeled as "cat" and hundreds of photos labeled as "dog". The algorithm learns to distinguish between cats and dogs and can subsequently be used to identify them in new, unlabeled images. The algorithm itself doesn't understand what a cat or a dog is, but when given a new photograph it can decide which category it aligns with, and how closely it aligns with it. This approach is great when there are identifiable categories such as regular email vs spam messages, or medical diagnoses comparing typical and atypical scans.

Unsupervised learning, on the other hand, involves unlabelled data. The algorithm tries to identify patterns and relationships based on the data given to it. The algorithm still learns to distinguish between groups to make predictions, but the groups themselves are chosen by the algorithm and are not really available for the user to read and understand. The algorithm becomes good at grouping in a way that humans might not think of. For example, unsupervised learning can be used to create groups of customers who have similar shopping habits and respond in a certain way to sales. It can also be used in fraud detection to help determine when there is suspicious activity that is outside of normal activity.

Regardless of the industry, AI is mostly being used to improve efficiency. In healthcare, we can use AI to diagnose diseases and predict the outcomes of various treatment plans. Retail uses AI systems to enhance inventory management and to make personalized recommendations. The customer service industry is using chatbots and virtual assistants powered by AI to help manage long wait times.

There are many advantages and disadvantages to using AI. AI systems are efficient and can process and analyze data much faster than people can. AI can automate routine tasks, freeing up workers to work on more complex tasks. In certain cases, AI systems can be less prone to making mistakes. This is especially true of repetitive tasks where human error tends to be high.

Of course, AI is not without its drawbacks as well. AI systems require large *datasets* to be trained, which requires people to collect the data. Then, in the case of supervised learning, it still needs to be labeled which can be a tedious task. AI systems can also use up a lot of resources compared to more traditional methods. The carbon footprint of training and using some of the popular AI models is staggering.[26] This is something that cannot be ignored in today's environmentally focused world. AI models are also only as good as the data used to train it. There is a lot of unintentional bias in the data which can translate to bias in our AI systems. For example, if our medical data is collected from people who can afford medical care, then our model will be biased against those who cannot.[27] We have to keep ethical concerns in mind when developing models and determine how and when they will be used.

Python is a leading language for developing and implementing AI and machine learning. There are many libraries that are available, such as TensorFlow, Keras, and scikit-learn that make it

---

26. Wu, Carole-Jean, Ramya Raghavendra, Udit Gupta, Bilge Acun, Newsha Ardalani, Kiwan Maeng, Gloria Chang, Fiona Aga, Jinshi Huang, Charles Bai, Michael Gschwind, Anurag Gupta, Myle Ott, Anastasia Melnikov, Salvatore Candido, David Brooks, Geeta Chauhan, Benjamin Lee, Hsien-Hsin Lee, Bugra Akyildiz, Maximilian Balandat, Joe Spisak, Ravi Jain, Mike Rabbat, and Kim Hazelwood. "Sustainable AI: Environmental Implications, Challenges and Opportunities." In *Proceedings of Machine Learning and Systems 4 (MLSys 2022)*, 2022.

27. Nelson, Gregory S. "Bias in artificial intelligence." North Carolina medical journal 80, no. 4 (2019): 220-222.

easy to get started with machine learning while still being useful for experienced programmers. We've already seen first-hand how easy it is to get started with Python's syntax and have experience installing and importing libraries, so we have the foundations to investigate any of these libraries further to see what they have to offer a novice programmer.

9.2 Internet of Things (IoT)

Whether we are aware of it or not, we are already taking part in the *Internet of Things (IoT)*. IoT refers to the vast network of devices that can communicate and exchange data through the internet. A smartphone can serve both as an IoT device and as a hub for other IoT devices as we can use them to monitor and control other devices through apps.

Wearable techs such as fitness trackers, smartwatches, and health monitors use sensors to collect data about their users and their activities and then transmit that information to either a server or directly to the user's smartphone. However, the concept can go much further than that. A health monitor could be set up to detect changes in heart activity or to detect falls and then automatically call for assistance.

Around the home more IoT devices are popping up. Smart thermostats can be set up to be controlled on an app from a smartphone or computer, but can also use location data to determine the optimal times to adjust heating and cooling to save energy without compromising comfort. Many people now have internet-connected doorbell cameras and video surveillance around their homes which can alert them of activity around the home. Smart lighting can be set up to work on a schedule or integrated with apps or voice assistants. Since many people check their phones first thing in the morning and stop using them last thing at night, it is easy to imagine a home that automatically syncs to a person's routine based on their phone activity.

The Internet of Things is not limited to individual needs. Across various industries, assets can be tagged with trackers to prevent theft or loss. This could be used for tracking livestock, delivery trucks, or expensive hospital equipment. Sensors can be used to notify when extra attention needs to be paid to a particular part of an operation. Smart garbage bins can notify waste collection services when they need to be collected and a computer-generated route for the day could be implemented, rather than a wasteful daily route. Soil monitoring could allow for more targeted crop maintenance, allowing water and fertilizer to be dispensed only as needed for better crop yield while being more efficient. Real-time tracking and collection of patient vitals could not only improve patient care but could also cut down on some of the necessary rounds for nurses. These technologies are not the future, they are here now and will continue to be improved upon.

Since IoT goes beyond working with just a traditional computer, a Python programmer would need a little more equipment to get started. Microcontrollers are small computing devices that can be used to control other devices. These can be hardwired in, or controlled in an IoT way. In sticking with Python as our main focus, the Raspberry PI is a small, affordable computer that can be programmed with Python, as well as other languages. It runs its own operating system and can be interfaced with many sensors and devices including DC motors and servos, making it a great entry point into IoT.

9.3 Web Scraping: An Introduction to Extracting Data from Websites

Whether it is for data analysis, research, or application use, data is an important commodity. *Web scraping* is the process of automatically extracting data from websites. The internet is a vast repository of information but manually collecting this data is time-consuming. Web scraping makes it possible to extract this data for our own purposes in a quick, cost-effective manner.

We can use Python to write programs that can collect the specific information that we want to harvest from various websites. The necessary libraries for web scraping include:

- **Requests:** Makes HTTP requests to fetch web pages.

- **BeautifulSoup:** Parses HTML documents to navigate through the structure of web pages to find the data we need.

- **Scrapy:** Handles complex tasks like following links and scraping the data. It's designed for large-scale operations.

Without going into too much detail, websites are built using HTML, which is Hypertext Markup Language. This provides the structure of content on the web page. The Document Object Model, or DOM, represents the structure of an HTML document. We navigate the DOM to find and extract the elements we want to scrape.

The general process is to use the "Requests" library to make an HTTP request to the server that hosts the web page. The server will then return the HTML content to the Python script. Once the HTML content is returned, the "BeautifulSoup" library can be used to parse it and navigate the DOM, extracting the elements based on the information within the structure.

While web scraping can be a powerful tool, it is important to be aware of the ethical, and possibly legal, implications of web scraping. Some websites have terms of service that explicitly prohibit scraping. Other web pages may have a "robots.txt" file that gives instructions on what is allowed, and not allowed, to be scrapped. These "robots.txt" files can be found by adding "/robots.txt" at the end of the web page's URL. For example, if we wanted to scrape information from Google, we should first check www.google.com/robots.txt. A segment of the file is shown below:

A portion of Google's "robots.txt" file

```
User-agent: *
Disallow: /search
Allow: /search/about
Allow: /search/static
Allow: /search/howsearchworks
Disallow: /sdch
Disallow: /groups
Disallow: /index.html?
Disallow: /?
Allow: /?hl=
Disallow: /?hl=*&
Allow: /?hl=*&gws_rd=ssl$
Disallow: /?hl=*&*&gws_rd=ssl
Allow: /?gws_rd=ssl$
Allow: /?pt1=true$
Disallow: /imgres
Disallow: /u/
Disallow: /preferences
Disallow: /setprefs
Disallow: /default
Disallow: /m?
Disallow: /m/
Allow:    /m/finance
```

Python libraries do not necessarily check for these files and certainly do not know the terms of service, so it is up to us to know what is appropriate to scrape. Once we have determined that we are allowed to scrape the data, we have to be aware that our Python programs could very easily disrupt a website by requesting too much information in a short period of time. When designing a scraping program, we need to add delays to mimic the way a person would use the website. Some pages may specifically give rate limits in their terms of service, but we should add delays regardless.

The other major consideration is what we are intending to use the data for. There are many legitimate cases for web scraping. If we ran a business with several competitors, we might want to compare our prices against their prices to stay competitive. We could manually load up their web pages periodically and check the prices, but this would be time-consuming, especially if we had hundreds or thousands of products to check. As long as their pages allow scraping, we could write a program that could take the product pricing data from each of our competitors weekly and give us a report of products that we price higher or lower. If we spread out the requests, there will be no disruptions to their sites and we will gain valuable insights without the manual hassle. A less legitimate case for web scraping would be to scrape the competitors' pages for email or social media contact information and then use that information for spamming them with messages. While gathering contact information is fine and could have a legitimate use, this is an unethical use of scraping.

There can also be legal implications as well. In 2008, Power Ventures was sued by Facebook for using automated scripts to collect information from their site, as well as using another user's Facebook accounts with authorization from Facebook. This was a violation of the terms of service.[28] It may be tempting to think that since we can legally access information manually on a computer,

---

28. United States Court of Appeals for the Ninth Circuit. Facebook V. Vachani. No. 13-17154, 2016. Accessed July 12, 2016. https://cdn.ca9.uscourts.gov/datastore/opinions/2016/07/12/13-17102.pdf.

automating the process through scraping would follow the same legal rules. However, this is not true. Always make sure to review a website's terms of service before engaging in data scraping.

9.4 Web Frameworks: Building Powerful Web Applications

It may be a little difficult to understand why we might want to build websites using Python without any experience in building websites. In the early days of the internet, websites tended to be fairly static. That is to say that when designed, the web page existed as an HTML file that did not change until another version of the site was uploaded. This is a simple method for making web pages and can still be useful when our content doesn't need to be changed frequently like a portfolio, personal blog, or an informational site, but this is simply not the way that most websites work nowadays.

Instead, most websites generate content dynamically. The pages themselves are built more as templates and draw data from databases based on user interaction. While these types of pages are more complicated to build, they can offer personalized experiences and interactivity in a way that static pages cannot. While the maintenance of the databases can be complex to maintain, the HTML of the page requires fewer changes since they are mainly templates. This is how social media sites can offer individual streams to users rather than a fixed landing page for all users. E-commerce sites can also benefit from this approach, only displaying products that are in stock and updating content as new products are added without having to redesign the page to accommodate the new items.

To simplify the task of setting up dynamic websites we use web *frameworks*. Web frameworks are pre-written code that is already set up to build web applications in a structured and efficient way, giving us solutions for handling common tasks such as handling HTTP requests, connecting to databases, and managing user authentication. This allows us to increase the speed of development by having reusable components and structures available to us rather than building them ourselves. This helps us focus on the features of the site rather than the nitpicky details. Frameworks also help keep things organized, making projects more maintainable, and also help with security features.

While using web frameworks to build dynamic sites is not only a Python language task, Python is an excellent choice for web development. As we've seen throughout this book, Python is easy to learn and read and has a large system of libraries that can be used to handle complex tasks. Since we also want to use Python to write machine learning code to analyze data collected by our web page, it is good to be able to write our applications in Python as well, avoiding the need to learn another language.

There are many different frameworks that can be used to power dynamic websites with Python, but two of the most common are Flask and Django. Of the two, Flask is more simplistic and easier to get started with. It is considered to be a more lightweight framework that is more minimalistic but has extensions that can be added to increase the features available. It is great for small projects that are relatively simple. While Flask supports extensions to add features, Django comes with all the features at the start. As a result, it can be a little overwhelming for beginners but it is ideal for large projects with complex requirements.

9.5 Cloud Computing Solutions

In any field, if you work with computers, you work with "the cloud". *Cloud computing* refers to delivering computer services over the Internet. Most of us are familiar with using cloud computing for file storage, but it also includes running servers, hosting databases, and handling networking. Before the popularity of cloud computing, businesses needed to physically set up their own computers and networking equipment to run their own servers. This required a lot of upfront costs to purchase the equipment and maintain it, along with the electricity to run and cool the equipment. As the business needs grew, additional equipment would need to be purchased to add more capacity to the system, making it difficult and expensive to scale.

Now with cloud computing, we can take advantage of the cloud computing options available from large tech corporations like Amazon, Microsoft, and Google. Instead of physical servers, virtual servers are used. They provide the same functions as physical servers but are software-based. This also means that they can be easily scaled as the business needs change, even throughout the day. If traffic increases, to a website, extra resources can be allocated to handle the load and then removed when the traffic decreases. Cloud services operate on pay-as-you-go models, so businesses only need to pay for the resources they use, making it cheaper than running their own servers. As an added benefit, since there is no one specific location for the servers, the information can be accessed globally.

There are several main uses for cloud computing:

Scalable Web Applications

Since cloud platforms can automatically scale to suit the varying traffic, they are well suited to web applications. This can ensure a consistent experience for users regardless of the number of users. For example, a ticket website would typically not need a lot of resources but during initial concert sales, they would need a lot of server resources.

Data Storage and Backup

A business needs to have secure and reliable data storage. Cloud storage provides the ability for businesses to store large amounts of data without having to worry about creating backups. Having data stored in the cloud also makes it accessible worldwide.

Big Data Analytics and Machine Learning

Previously, we discussed how big data could be used to build models and create business insights, however, all that data needs to be stored somewhere. Many cloud platforms provide tools to analyze this data as well as store it, enabling businesses to incorporate AI solutions into their operations without investing in the hardware required to create the models.

Once again Python's versatility and vast library ecosystem make it a powerful tool in cloud computing. Platforms like Amazon AWS, Microsoft Azure, and Google Cloud all support Python for server-side programming, enabling tasks such as data analysis, machine learning, and automation.

Quiz

1. **What is the purpose behind artificial intelligence?**
   a. To generate datasets
   b. To mimic human intelligence
   c. To perform simple routine tasks
   d. To replace humans in basic tasks

2. **Machine learning is a subset of which field?**
   a. Artificial intelligence
   b. Database management
   c. Network security
   d. Web development

3. **How is supervised learning different from unsupervised learning?**
   a. Supervised learning uses numerical data
   b. Supervised learning uses labeled data
   c. Unsupervised learning uses numerical data
   d. Unsupervised learning uses labeled data

4. **Michael is training a ML model but is concerned about bias in the model. What should he do to minimize the risk of bias?**
   a. Avoid using test data when training
   b. Ensure the data is representative and diverse
   c. Train on a much larger dataset
   d. Use a mix of labeled and unlabeled data

5. Which is an example of unsupervised learning?

    a. Classifying emails as spam

    b. Diagnosing diseases from medical images

    c. Grouping customers based on purchases

    d. Identifying cats from images

6. Which Python library is used with machine learning?

    a. BeautifulSoup

    b. Matplotlib

    c. NumPy

    d. TensorFlow

7. Which is a disadvantage of AI?

    a. It has no practical applications

    b. It is difficult to use

    c. It is inaccurate

    d. It requires large amounts of data

8. Which is a use case of IoT?

    a. Building dynamic websites

    b. Connecting household appliances to the Internet

    c. Developing mobile apps

    d. Writing desktop software

9. How can IoT benefit the healthcare industry?

    a. By automating surgeries

    b. By eliminating hospitals

    c. By providing real-time health information

    d. By replacing doctors

10. Which best describes connecting everyday devices to the internet?

    a. Artificial Intelligence

    b. Cloud Computing

    c. Internet of Things

    d. Machine Learning

Answers	1 – b	2 – a	3 – b	4 – b	5 – c
	6 – d	7 – d	8 –b	9 – c	10 – c

Chapter Summary

◆ AI mimics human intelligence, while ML develops algorithms for predictions.

◆ IoT connects devices to communicate and exchange data.

◆ Web scraping automates data extraction from websites but has possible ethical and legal implications.

◆ Python has several frameworks to simplify the development of dynamic websites.

◆ Cloud computing provides scalable, cost-effective services for businesses.

Chapter 10

Next Steps and Further Resources

In this chapter, we will explore the next steps to advance your Python journey. We'll investigate practical ways to build upon your skills as well as investigate potential career paths to pursu. We will also introduce several popular tools that would be beneficial to programmers who want to get serious about working with Python and other programming languages.

The key learning objectives of this chapter are:

- Identifying how to set goals and routines to build programming habits

- Identifying opportunities to practice programming

- Exploring career paths for programmers

- Identifying essential tools and resources to assist in programming

10.1 Continuing Your Python Journey

The journey to master programming does not end with one book. Learning Python is a continuous process and there are many paths available to continue expanding your skills. It is important to set achievable goals to stay focused and motivated. Goals should be specific, measurable, achievable, relevant, and time-bound. For instance, instead of simply wanting to "get better at Python," a more effective goal could be: "In two weeks, analyze a dataset using Pandas and create visualizations based on the data."

Working on small programs will help you develop basic skills before moving on to more advanced topics. Look for small problems that can be solved using programming and see if you can write a program to solve them. Even if the solution ends up being too complex right now, the process of thinking about the solution, breaking it into pieces, and writing some code will solidify your programming skills.

As you get more comfortable with the basics, consider learning more about complex *data structures and algorithms*. Understanding commonly used algorithms can help tackle problems that may seem impossible at the beginning of your programming journey. If you have an interest in web development or data science, it's a good idea to explore tutorials that align with your learning goals. You can even start looking into using Python for game development, computer vision, or generative artwork. The choice is up to you.

10.2 Building Programming Skills

Practice is the key to becoming a better programmer. Here are some suggestions to help you stay on track:

- **Daily coding:** Block out a set amount of time to dedicate to code. This could be for writing code, but it could also be watching online videos, reading another programmer's code, or participating in an online course. Even if you end up researching a new library for 30 minutes, getting into the habit of working regularly is helpful.

- **Project-Based Learning:** Choose a project that interests you and start working on it. As your skills grow you can tackle more advanced topics, and hopefully more interesting, projects. Use this as a way to build a portfolio of your projects.

- **Coding Communities:** Being part of a community, either online or in person, can be a great way to stay motivated and get support. There are many online forums and Discord servers where you can discuss programming issues. Local meetups and hackathons are becoming increasingly popular as well. A support network goes a long way.

- **Contributing to Open Source Projects:** There are many projects online that would benefit from an eager programmer looking to gain some experience. There can be some headaches in learning to work with Git, a version control software, but once you do, there is a network of programmers building amazing projects on sites like GitHub. Beginners can start small by improving documentation and helping to identify and fix small bugs,

and thanks to the version control software, there is no risk
to the main software if a mistake is made.

- **Coding Challenges:** Approach these with caution. Websites
  like LeetCode, HackerRank, and CodeSignal offer coding
  challenges, but they tend to be very algorithm-based and
  not overly beginner-friendly. They focus on interview style
  problems, which may not be the best way to learn as a
  beginner, but will certainly help you build your skills when
  you are ready.

10.3 What to Do When You Get Stuck

When programming, you can expect something to go wrong.
Making mistakes isn't something that goes away with experience,
but overcoming issues becomes much easier. Debugging is the
most important tool to diagnose and fix errors. We looked at
reading error messages back in Chapter 6 and it really is an
important tool. As you start to recognize the common error types
you will find that it becomes much quicker to pinpoint the source
of the error. Searching for the error online will also help determine
the right course of action.

If you still can't find a solution to the error and Chapter 6
doesn't lead you to the right solution, there are some other steps to
take. First, we can add extra `print` *statements* into our programs
to print out the values of *variables*, or to match the area of code that
is currently running. Printing variable values is an effective way
to confirm that they are changing as expected, while strategically
placing print statements to indicate your position in the code can
help you track the program's flow. Sometimes it is something as

simple as a *function* not being called or a *loop* not being entered, and a few extra `print` statements can quickly identify the issue.

We can also isolate segments of code to see if they are working as expected. If the program is broken down into functions, test the functions separately and see if any errors can be spotted. We can also comment out sections of code to see if a particular line of code is causing an issue. This is problematic in a large program, but the error message can inform us as to where the problem might be occurring.

If a particular library or function is causing the issue, check the official documentation. The built-in functions and libraries that come with Python are very well-documented, and most of the popular libraries are also well-documented. It could be something as simple as an argument being passed out of order, or an incorrect data type being used.

Most IDEs also come with built-in debuggers which will step through code line by line to inspect the values of variables. Taking this slow route through a program is tedious, but it can point out errors that we may otherwise miss. We can also set specific breakpoints that we can skip to and investigate the program at that point as well, which is helpful if we have an idea of where the issue may be occurring.

Finally, we can turn to AI. Generative AI software like ChatGPT does a fairly good job of investigating code for some obvious mistakes that could be missed when skimming through for a mistake. It can also identify some logical errors if the original intent of the program is explained, which goes well beyond the ability of the error report generated by Python. Be careful however as sometimes it can miss the point and focus on the wrong details. It can even invent solutions that sound wonderful but simply do not exist. It is often quicker to investigate the problem through more traditional routes than to use AI.

10.4 Exploring Career Opportunities in Programming

Getting a job in programming doesn't need to be the end goal of learning to program, but programming skills can certainly open up a wide range of career opportunities. The most obvious area is software development. It involves designing, coding, testing, and maintaining software applications. This could be on software meant to run on mobile devices, desktops, or both. Python is a great start for software development, but depending on the development environment, other languages might be required. It would be an excellent idea to build a portfolio and if you are serious about developing in Python, getting certified would be a great idea. There are a variety of options for certification, but the Python Institute is a reputable organization with options for beginners.

Data science and analytics, as we investigated in Chapter 7, is a rapidly growing field involving machine learning, data visualization, and data analysis. This tends to be more mathematically focused than software development and basic knowledge in statistics would be important. Besides the Python libraries that we already investigated, Jupyter Notebook is a standard tool for data analysis. Jupyter Notebook runs Python commands in cells instead of executing an entire script at once. It's a bit of a different workflow, but it is fairly easy to get into. There is an online version at https://jupyter.org and it can also be integrated into Visual Studio Code. Platforms like Kaggle (https://

www.kaggle.com/) host datasets that can be used in our projects. They also host coding challenges to help with skill building.

If web development sounds like a better fit, HTML and CSS are essential for working with websites. These are essential for *frontend* development, which is the side of the web that users see. The backend is where most of the coding comes into play and happens behind the scenes. *Frameworks* like Django and Flask can be used if we want to continue with Python, but Node.js is a JavaScript option as well. Many programmers choose to work on both frontend and backend, which we call *full-stack*. Building and deploying web applications would be a great way to build your skills for a career in web development.

Cybersecurity involves protecting the data contained in systems and networks from digital attacks. This involves both programming skills and security principles. Cybersecurity is an exciting and ever evolving field. An interesting way to build security skills is to practice *ethical hacking*. Ethical hacking involves having permission to access computer systems and sensitive data in the same way that a *hacker* would try to access them. By understanding how people gain unlawful access to secure information, ethical hackers can transition into cybersecurity. Courses in ethical hacking are becoming more popular and there are sites that offer hacking simulations.

Programming skills can also come in handy in other areas, especially when combined with other professional skills. Technical writing, in the form of books, blogs, and tutorials is a great way to combine technical skills with communication skills. *UX (user experience)* and *UI (user interface)* consider how users interact with technology. This combines tech skills with design skills. Business skills and tech skills can be used together in business analysis to help organizations optimize their operations.

10.5 Recommended Tools and Resources

If you've followed along with the examples in this book using an online IDE, now is an excellent time to install Python on your own device and install an IDE of your own. There is no one best IDE and people have their own preferences. A popular choice among those starting out is Visual Studio Code. It is extremely versatile and, through extensions, can support multiple programming languages. If you are looking for something a little more Python-specific, PyCharm is specifically tailored for Python. It offers a lot of powerful tools that can make working on complex projects more streamlined. If you want a simple editor with just the necessary tools, Thonny is a Python-specific IDE which is very straightforward. It might not be the best for large projects but is excellent for just starting out. Jupyter Notebook is an excellent choice if you intend to work with data and machine learning. It can be installed on its own or as an extension for Visual Studio Code.

Another popular tool when coding is Git. Git is a version control system that tracks changes in your files and makes branches when you want to try out a new feature without affecting the rest of your project. The files and the history of changes are stored as a repository, often called a "repo" for short. Git can even roll back changes if something goes wrong, so you never have to worry about losing your progress. GitHub is a popular platform for hosting repositories and provides extra tools for working collaboratively with others. It is an excellent place to showcase the work you are creating and a great place to find open-source projects to contribute to.

For writing high-quality code, you may want to look into using a linter, such as pylint. A linter is a tool that not only analyzes code for potential errors but also checks to ensure that coding standards are followed. Using a linter can help develop good coding habits like writing clean and maintainable code.

In addition to these features, pylint also detects "code smells" which are patterns that may indicate problems in your code that may not cause errors but can lead to deeper issues. This includes things such as complex functions, redundant code, and potential performance issues. If your code smells "bad", pylint can help you address these issues before they lead to bigger problems. Many IDEs support Pylint and it can also be run from the command prompt. Pylint can be installed using pip by running the command "pip install pylint".

Another area to investigate is writing proper documentation. Documentation is a set of materials that describes the functionality, usage, and structure of the programs that you write. Effective documentation is essential for understanding, using, and maintaining programs. We have already investigated an important step in the documentation process in Chapter 4 when we looked at docstrings.

Docstrings enable us to provide detailed descriptions of the functions and classes we write directly within the code. Docstrings are limited to the code itself and do not offer a comprehensive overview of the entire project.

Fortunately, tools such as Sphinx can generate documentation directly from the docstrings in our codes. Sphinx can format this documentation into various formats such as PDFs or HTML websites. This makes it more accessible and useful for other audiences besides programmers. Sphinx can be installed with pip by running the command "pip install sphinx".

There are many online learning platforms that offer tutorials and courses to expand your programming knowledge. YouTube has countless hours of Python tutorials, although the quality varies from creator to creator, but with a little patience, you can find someone who matches your learning style. freeCodeCamp, https://www.freecodecamp.org/, offers free courses with certifications in a variety of programming languages including Python and there are many paid options such as Coursera, Udacity, LinkedIn Learning, and countless others, which you may want to investigate as well. Before entering into a paid option, be sure to understand what it will cost and what you will actually receive at the end. Many paid options will offer free trials so you can determine what works best for you.

As you continue on your programming journey, remember that learning is an ongoing process. There will be challenges along the way, but you have been given the tools to overcome the obstacles and learn from them. As you build your coding skills and grow as a programmer, you can decide which way your path winds. Whether you aim for data science, game development, or software development, the journey is yours to enjoy.

Quiz

1. **Frank wants to improve his Python skills. Which is a specific and achievable goal for him?**

   a. Become a Python expert in three weeks

   b. Build a web app with Flask in two weeks

   c. Getting better at Python

   d. Learn everything about Python

2. **What is the benefit of daily coding practice?**

   a. It ensures mastery of Python

   b. It guarantees the elimination of mistakes

   c. It helps establish consistent programming habits

   d. It replaces the need for coding challenges

3. **How can Jessica gain experience programming while becoming involved in a supportive community?**

   a. Contributing to open-source projects

   b. Focusing on Python and avoiding Git

   c. Reading additional books on Python

   d. Working on a daily coding exercise

4. **Amari wants to enhance his data analysis skills by mastering Pandas and Matplotlib. What approach should he take?**

   a. Analyze real-world datasets and solve practical problems

   b. Chose only one library to focus on to become an expert

   c. Memorize the syntax and basic functions of both libraries

   d. Prioritize watching tutorial videos over daily practice

5. **If the error message does not help a programmer solve an error, what should they do?**

   a. Add additional "print" statements with descriptions

   b. Give up and start another project

   c. Ignore the error and continue coding

   d. Rewrite the program from scratch

6. **Which tools step through code line by line to inspect the values of variables?**

   a. Code editors

   b. Debuggers

   c. Spreadsheets

   d. Version control

7. **A function imported from a specific library is causing issues in Eliana's code. What should she do?**

   a. Check the official documentation for the library

   b. Delete the function and find an alternative method

   c. Paste the code into an AI software and ask for a solution

   d. Stop using the library and code her own version of the function

8. **Which field involves designing, coding, testing, and maintaining software applications?**

   a. Data Science

   b. Cybersecurity

   c. Software development

   d. Web development

9. **What does ethical hacking involve?**

    a. Analyzing datasets

    b. Building secure websites

    c. Hacking into systems without permission

    d. Using hacking techniques to check for vulnerabilities

10. **Jasmine enjoys programming but is more interested in creating user-friendly interfaces. Which career should she explore?**

    a. Backend developer

    b. Database administrator

    c. Data scientist

    d. UX / UI designer

Answers	1 – b	2 – c	3 – a	4 – a	5 – a
	6 – b	7 – a	8 – c	9 – d	10 – d

Chapter Summary

◆ Setting goals that are specific, measurable, achievable, relevant, and time-bound helps keep programmers focused.

◆ Programming skills can be improved by working on personal projects or contributing to open-source projects.

◆ There are a variety of debugging techniques and supportive communities of programmers.

◆ There are a variety of careers in software, not all of which involve simply writing code.

◆ Many software programs exist to help programmers including IDEs, linters, documentation generators, and version control software.

Glossary

Abstraction: Hiding complex details of a system. Only necessary parts are exposed.

Algorithm: A step-by-step process for solving a problem or completing a task.

Algorithm Complexity: The time to run and the memory required for an algorithm to execute, based on the input size.

Argument: A value that is passed to a function when it is called.

Artificial Intelligence (AI): Mimicking human intelligence with machines.

Attribute: A variable associated with a class/object.

Attribute Error (AttributeError): An error that occurs when trying to access an attribute that does not belong to that object.

Backend development: The development of websites specifically involving the databases and servers.

Bias: Error introduced in a machine learning model by limited data or oversimplification of real-world problems.

Big data: Large data sets that are too large for traditional analysis, but can be analyzed by computers.

Boolean: A data type that can only be "True" or "False".

Child class: A class that inherits attributes and methods from a parent class.

Class: A template for creating objects, including methods and attributes.

Cloud computing: Computer services that are delivered over the internet, including storage, processing, and software.

Comma Separated Value (CSV) Files: A plain text format for representing tabular data.

Composition: When a class is made up of one or more objects.

Computer vision: An AI field where computers are trained to interpret visual data.

Conditions / Conditional Statement: Expressions in programming that evaluate at either true or false. Used to make decisions in code.

Constraints: Limitations and restrictions defined for a particular problem situation.

Constructor: A special method of a class that is called when an instance is created. Used to initialize attributes.

Creative coding: Writing code to produce expressive, artistic works instead of functional programs.

DataFrame: Two-dimensional tabular data used with the pandas library.

Dataset: A collection of information meant to be analyzed.

Data structure: A format for organizing and storing data efficiently.

Decrement: Decreasing the value of a variable by an amount, typically 1.

Deep learning: A subset of machine learning involving neural networks.

Dictionary: A mutable data structure that holds an ordered collection of key-value pairs.

Difference: The elements present in one set, but not in another.

Docstring: Documenting a specific segment of code, such as a module, class, or function.

Encapsulate: Containing most of the logic and data handling within a single object or class.

Encapsulation: Bundling attributes and methods in a class and restricting direct access to an object's components.

Edge Case: A rare situation that occurs at the extremes of parameters and needs to be specifically tested to avoid problems.

Error: An issue in a program that causes it to stop unexpectedly, or to produce incorrect results.

Escape character: In Python, a backslash ("\") followed by a character with a special meaning, such as "\n" for new line, or to remove the special use of a character, such as "\\" to indicate that we want a backslash and not an escape character.

Ethical Concerns: The moral implications and responsibilities to be considered when developing programs and using technology.

Ethical Hacking: Deliberately breaking into computer systems to find weaknesses so they can be made more secure.

Exception: An event that disrupts the normal flow of a problem due to errors during runtime.

F-strings: Formatted strings that allow variables and expressions to be embedded directly into a string.

Finally: A block of code in a try-except block that runs whether an exception occurred or not.

Float / Floating Points: A data type of represents numbers with fractional or decimal parts.

Flowchart: A visual representation of an algorithm or computer program.

For loop: A loop that iterates over a sequence, such as a range of numbers. Runs a set number of times.

Framework: A platform for developing software applications.

Frontend development: The development of websites specifically involving the parts that users see and interact with.

Full-stack development: The development of websites involving both the server-side and user-facing parts.

Functions: Blocks of reusable code that perform a specific task. Defined by the "def" keyword in Python.

Generative art: Art that is created using systems such as algorithms, computer programs, or mathematical models.

Getter: A method that retrieves or accesses an attribute of an object.

Global variables: Variables that are defined outside of any function and can be accessed anywhere in the code.

Hackers: Individuals who use technical knowledge to exploit weaknesses in computer systems.

Immutable: An object whose value cannot be modified after creation.

Increment: Increasing a variable by an amount, typically 1.

Indentation: Represented in Python by a number of spaces, typically 2 or 4, or a single tab. Indentation indicates a block of code.

Index: The position of an item in an ordered collection.

Index error (IndexError): An error that occurs when trying to access an index that is outside the bounds of an ordered collection.

Inheritance: A method by which child classes inherit attributes and methods from their parent class.

Instance: An individual object created by a class.

Integer: A data type representing positive and negative numbers without decimal or fractional parts.

Internet of Things (IoT): The network of objects with sensors and software that connect and exchange data over the internet.

Intersection: The common elements present in two or more sets.

Iterate: Process through a sequence one at a time, commonly through loops.

Key-value pair: Used in dictionaries. An association where a key is mapped to a value.

Key error (KeyError): An error that occurs when trying to access a key that doesn't exist.

Library: A collection of pre-written code that programmers can use to add functionality to their own code.

List: A mutable data structure that holds an ordered collection of items.

Local variables: Variables defined within a function that cannot be accessed outside that function.

Loops: Constructs that allow for the repeated execution of a block of code.

Machine Learning: A branch of AI that uses data to learn and make decisions.

Method: A function defined within a class.

Method overriding: Where a child class provides the same method as a parent class, the child method overrides the parents.

Microcontroller: A small computer or integrated circuit designed to handle inputs and outputs, typically with programming.

Mixed case (mixed case): A way of avoiding spaces when writing names in programming.

Modular programming: A framework that emphasizes breaking a program into independent modules.

Mutable: Values that can be changed after they are created.

Null: A special value indicating that a variable does not have a value.

Object: An instance of a class. Contains attributes and methods defined by the class.

Object-oriented programming (OOP): A framework which emphasizes using objects.

Parameter: A variable used when defining a function. It is a placeholder for a value to be passed into the function.

Parent class: A child from which children classes inherit information.

Parse: Converting data into a structured format that a program can understand.

Polymorphism: The ability of classes to have different methods based on their specific class.

Private attribute: An attribute that should only be accessed within its own class. Indicated by two underscores.

Procedural programming: A framework where functions are the primary method of structuring code.

Programmatic Thinking: A structured approach to problem-solving by breaking problems into smaller, more manageable parts and creating algorithms to solve them.

Programming: The act of writing code and developing solutions.

Protected attribute: An attribute that should only be accessed within its own class and subclasses. Indicated by one underscore.

Pseudocode: A plain language representation of an algorithm or computer program.

Public attribute: An attribute that can be accessed from anywhere.

Python: A high-level computer programming language, known for its readability and wide range of uses.

Raise: A command used to explicitly trigger an exception.

Refactor: Restructuring existing code to improve its readability and maintainability, without changing its behavior.

Script: A program written in a coding language that is typically executed without compiling.

Scope: Where a variable is defined and can be accessed.

Series: One-dimensional data, like a row or column, is used with the pandas library.

Servers: Computers or systems that provide resources, data, and services over a network

Set: An unordered collection of unique items.

Setter: A method used to set the value of a protected or private attribute.

Statement: An instruction in a program that performs a specific task or operation.

String: A data type which is a sequence of characters surrounded by quotation marks.

Subclass: Inherits from a parent class.

Superclass: A class with some parents wanted.

Supervised learning: A type of machine learning where the model is trained on labeled data.

Syntax: The set of rules that defines how programming interprets commands.

Traceback: An error report containing the function calls made leading up to the error.

Try-except: A block structure used to handle exceptions. The "try" block is executed and if there is an exception, it stops and the "except" block runs instead.

Tuple: An immutable data structure that holds an ordered collection of items.

Union: Combining all the elements from two or more sets, excluding duplicates.

Unsupervised Learning: A type of machine learning where the model is trained on unlabeled data.

User experience (UX): The overall experience of a user using a product, often a website or application.

User interface (UI): How a user interacts with a computer system or software, including screens, pages, and visual elements.

Value error (ValueError): An error that occurs when a function receives an inappropriate value.

Variable: A container for data, associated with a name, which may be changed during a program.

Web scraping: The process of extracting data from websites.

While loop: A loop that continues while a condition is true. Runs an indeterminate number of times.

Wildcard character: A symbol used to replace one or more characters. In Python, it is an asterisk.

Bibliography

California State Legislature. California Consumer Privacy Act of 2018, California Civil Code, Division 3, Part 4, Title 1.81.5. Accessed June 29, 2024.

Cadwalladr, Carole, and Emma Graham-Harrison. "Revealed: 50 Million Facebook Profiles Harvested for Cambridge Analytica in Major Data Breach." The Guardian, March 17, 2018. https://www.theguardian.com/news/2018/mar/17/cambridge-analytica-facebook-influence-us-election.

Dalbey, John. "Pseudocode Standard." Accessed March 20, 2024. https://users.csc.calpoly.edu/~jdalbey/SWE/pdl_std.htm.

Data.gov. "Privacy and Website Policies." Accessed July 2, 2024. https://data.gov/privacy-policy/.

Didssph. "A red, blue, and yellow ceramic figurine," February 22, 2021. Unsplash. https://unsplash.com/photos/red-blue-and-yellow-ceramic-figurine-PB80D_B4g7c.

Eliason, Kenny. "Blue case photo," February 1, 2017. Unsplash. https://unsplash.com/photos/black-case-3MGbXrdV8Mo.

European Parliament and Council of the European Union. Regulation (EU) 2016/679 of the European Parliament and of the Council of 27 April 2016 on the Protection of Natural Persons with regard to the Processing of Personal Data and on the Free Movement of Such Data, and Repealing Directive 95/46/EC (General Data Protection Regulation). Official Journal of the European Union L 119/1, May 4, 2016. Accessed June 29, 2024. https://eur-lex.europa.eu/legal-content/EN/TXT/PDF/?uri=CELEX:32016R0679.

Felisilda, Rafael Rex. "Chess Pieces on Chess Board," January 20, 2021. Unsplash. https://unsplash.com/photos/chess-pieces-on-chess-board-U_Kz2RnfFAk.

Goldstein, Zachary. "Five Stacked Books with Assorted Colors," July 5, 2019. Unsplash. https://unsplash.com/photos/five-stacked-books-Pf0e3GTr8P4.

Helgesen, Torbjørn. "A notepad with a green pen sitting on top of it," June 9, 2021. Unsplash. https://unsplash.com/photos/a-notepad-with-a-green-pen-sitting-on-top-of-it-C4FbCe4L_pw.

LeFebvre, Dan. "Gray Nest thermostat displaying at 63," December 19, 2018. Unsplash. https://unsplash.com/photos/gray-nest-thermostat-displaying-at-63-RFAHj4tI37Y.

Licensed Drivers, by State, Gender, and Age Group. Last modified May 8, 2024. Data.gov. https://catalog.data.gov/dataset/licensed-drivers-by-state-gender-and-age-group.

Lollixzc. "AI Hierarchy," August 19, 2022. Wikimedia Commons. https://commons.wikimedia.org/wiki/File:AI_hierarchy.svg.

Maryland Total Residential Sales 2010 - 2022 Zip Codes. Last modified March 22, 2024. Data.gov. https://catalog.data.gov/dataset/maryland-total-residential-sales-2010-2022-zip-codes.

Matplotlib. "Matplotlib Documentation – Matplotlib 3.9.0 Documentation." Accessed July 3, 2024. https://matplotlib.org/stable/.

Matplotlib. "matplotlib.lines.Line2D – Matplotlib 3.9.0 documentation." Accessed July 3, 2024. https://matplotlib.org/stable/api/_as_gen/matplotlib.lines.Line2D.html#matplotlib.lines.Line2D. set_linestyle.

Matplotlib. "matplotlib.markers – Matplotlib 3.9.0 documentation." Accessed July 3, 2024. https:// matplotlib.org/stable/api/markers_api.html#module-matplotlib.markers.

Matplotlib. "Specifying colors – Matplotlib 3.9.0 documentation." Accessed July 3, 2024. https:// matplotlib.org/stable/users/explain/colors/colors.html#sphx-glr-users-explain-colors-co.

NASA. "Aerial photography of city during nighttime," November 5, 2015. Unsplash. https:// unsplash.com/photos/aerial-photography-of-city-during-night-time-1lfI7wkGWZ4.

Nelson, Gregory S. "Bias in Artificial Intelligence." North Carolina Medical Journal 80, no. 4 (2019): 220-222.

OpenAI. "Introducing ChatGPT." Published November 30, 2022. https://openai.com/index/chatgpt/.

Pahalyants, Vartan. "Netflix: A Streaming Giant's Big Data Approach to Entertainment." Accessed June 30, 2024. https://d3.harvard.edu/platform-digit/submission/netflix-a-streaming-giants-big-data-approach-to-entertainment/.

Pandas. "pandas.DataFrame.plot – pandas 2.2.2 Documentation." Accessed July 3, 2024. https:// pandas.pydata.org/docs/reference/api/pandas.DataFrame.plot.html.

PEP 8, "PEP 8 - Style Guide for Python Code," Python.org, accessed August 1, 2024, https://peps. python.org/pep-0008/.

Python Documentation. "3. Data Model – Python 3.12.4 Documentation." Accessed June 16, 2024. https://docs.python.org/3/reference/datamodel.html.

Python Documentation. "Built-in Exceptions – Python 3.12.4." Accessed June 29, 2024. https://docs. python.org/3/library/exceptions.html.

Python Documentation. "Built-in Functions – Python 3.12.3 Documentation." Accessed April 21, 2024. https://docs.python.org/3/library/functions.html.

Python Documentation. "Data Structures – Python 3.12.3 Documentation." Accessed May 24, 2024. https://docs.python.org/3/tutorial/datastructures.html.

Python Documentation. "What's New in Python 3.7." Accessed May 23, 2024. https://docs.python. org/3.7/whatsnew/3.7.html.

Python Documentation. "What's New in Python 3.11 – Python 3.11.8 Documentation." Accessed June 23, 2024. https://docs.python.org/3.11/whatsnew/3.11.html.

Samoili, Sofia, Marta Lopez Cobo, Boban Delipetrev, Francesca Martinez-Plumed, Eduardo Gomez Gutierrez, and Giuditta De Prato. AI Watch. Defining Artificial Intelligence 2.0. EUR 30873 EN. Luxembourg: Publications Office of the European Union, 2021. ISBN 978-92-76-42648-6. doi:10.2760/019901. JRC126426.

Schibelius, Lisa, Amanda Ross, and Andrew Katz. "An Empirical Study of Programming Languages Specified in Engineering Job Postings." American Society for Engineering Education, 2022.

Spiske, Markus. "Weekend sale men/women up to 70% off," November 1, 2019. Unsplash. https://unsplash.com/photos/weekend-sale-signage-5UJbKYUjFCk.

Stéphane V. "Starbucks: From Coffee Machines to Machine Learning." Accessed June 30, 2024. https://d3.harvard.edu/platform-digit/submission/starbucks-from-coffee-machines-to-machine-learning/.

TIOBE Software BV. "TIOBE Index for March 2024." Accessed March 12, 2024. https://www.tiobe.com/tiobe-index/.

United States Court of Appeals for the Ninth Circuit. Facebook v. Vachani. No. 13-17154, 2016. Accessed July 12, 2016. https://cdn.ca9.uscourts.gov/datastore/opinions/2016/07/12/13-17102.pdf.

UX Indonesia. "Design Thinking," April 21, 2020. Unsplash. https://unsplash.com/photos/person-writing-on-white-paper-qC2n6RQU4Vw.

World Economic Forum. "Future of Jobs Report 2023 – Insight Report May 2023." Published April 30, 2023. https://www3.weforum.org/docs/WEF_Future_of_Jobs_2023.pdf.

"Worldwide Interest in the Search Term 'AI'," Google Trends. Accessed June 30, 2024. https://www.google.com/trends.

Wu, Carole-Jean, Ramya Raghavendra, Udit Gupta, Bilge Acun, Newsha Ardalani, Kiwan Maeng, Gloria Chang, Fiona Aga, Jinshi Huang, Charles Bai, Michael Gschwind, Anurag Gupta, Myle Ott, Anastasia Melnikov, Salvatore Candido, David Brooks, Geeta Chauhan, Benjamin Lee, Hsien-Hsin Lee, Bugra Akyildiz, Maximilian Balandat, Joe Spisak, Ravi Jain, Mike Rabbat, and Kim Hazelwood. "Sustainable AI: Environmental Implications, Challenges and Opportunities." In Proceedings of Machine Learning and Systems 4 (MLSys 2022), 2022. https://proceedings.mlsys.org/paper_files/paper/2022/hash/462211f67c7d858f663355eff93b745e-Abstract.html.

Notes